MW01629862

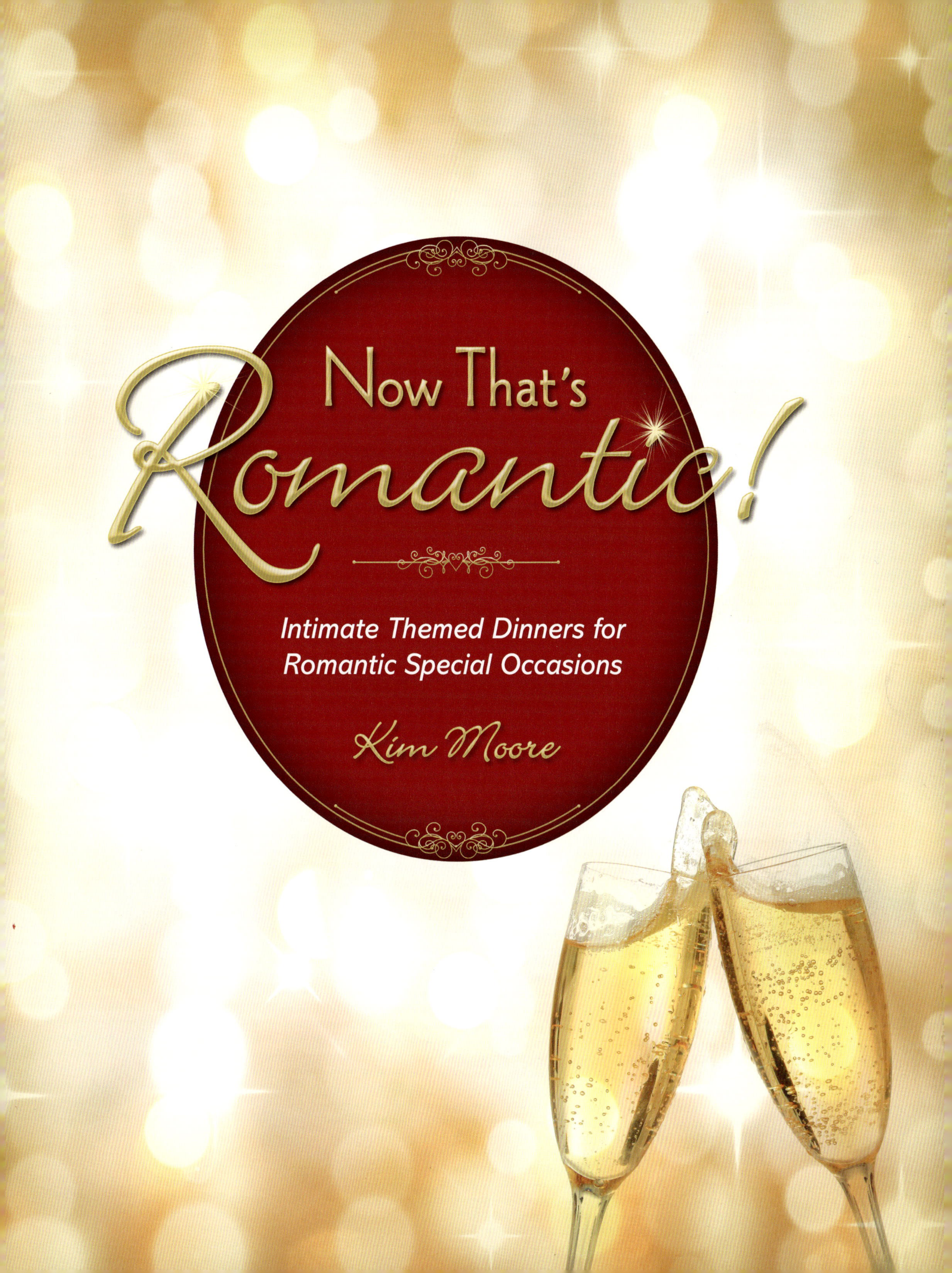

Now That's
Romantic!
Intimate Themed Dinners for
Romantic Special Occasions
Kim Moore

To Doug,
My One and Only

Your unconditional love, patience and encouragement inspired every word of this book. Consider it the world's longest love letter.

To Austin

You're not only beautiful on the outside, you're beautiful on the inside. You have always been mature and disciplined beyond your years. I am proud to call you my son.

To Tyler

My huge son with an equally huge heart. Your tenacity will take you far in life. I cherish our talks and bantering texts. You make me smile.

To Mom

Thank you for the heart-shaped Valentine's Day cakes, Easter basket cakes, Halloween finger cookies and playing "dress-up." You definitely instilled your love of entertaining and thinking outside the box in me. See what you started?

Acknowledgements

I'd like to say thank you to:

All the beautiful women in my Word Weavers group, you have been a constant source of knowledge and encouragement. A special thank you to Sharron, Jan, Kat and Sheryl for your time and input throughout this lengthy process.

Karen Andrews and Mary Rathman for putting the quotes and hyphens in their place.

Robert of Robert Crum Photography, for capturing the magic.

My sister Tammy, who not only allowed the Pirates to invade her home, she welcomed them.

Mike Ruvolo, for an awesome logo.

Peri Gabriel of Knockout Design, few people meet my expectations—you exceeded them.

Joel Osteen, whom I've never met, but your books and lessons kept me going.

I couldn't have done it without any of you.

Contents

Introduction

*A*re you going through the same romantic rituals year after year? Valentine's Day? Anniversaries? Birthdays? Can you anticipate every move before it happens? No imagination, no passion, no thrill and most of all—*no fun*.

How many times have you racked your brain trying to come up with something new and exciting? But what? And where do you find it?

First, you turn on your computer and fire up the search engines. Within seconds, page after page of websites scroll down the screen, but one by one your hopes fade as you realize it's just more of the same lame stuff. No love gurus here.

Next, you ask a couple of friends if they have any ideas to share. Nope. They're in the same boat you're in.

Weary and frustrated, you scour through books and magazines at your local bookstore or library. Unless you're fond of cooking, your search is futile. The shelves are chock-full of romantic and aphrodisiac cookbooks. But what about those of us who are *culinarily challenged* or just plain hate to cook?

Days fly by, time runs out and you end up doing the same old thing *again*—*another ordinary special occasion.*

> Another ordinary special occasion.

Having been in that situation more times than I'd like to admit, and refusing to believe the best days of our marriage were behind us, I knew something had to change. As a professional decorator, I decided to put my experience to use in an intimate way. I began designing what I now call *"romantic roomscapes."* As each one emerged, it possessed a unique mood and personality all its own—some playful and seductive, others wild and exotic.

Don't get me wrong. I didn't reinvent the wheel; I just came up with a new and improved wheel. In other words, I still do the candle thing, the sexy clothes and the music thing; I just do them on steroids.

Take a peek…

Drift away to the crystal azure waters of the Caribbean… Feel the balmy breezes caress your skin as they whisper through palm trees and the white linens of your cabana… Let the easy-going rhythm of steel drums melt your worries… Delicate orchids adorn your table as you savor an icy Margarita and succulent crab cakes.

Or…

Colorful rose petals beckon the way to a room brimming with flickering firelight, the fragrance of roses and the sounds of tender love songs.

But that's just the beginning. The trail leads on and encircles a velvety white, heart-shaped bearskin rug lying in the warm radiance of a brilliant fire. Beside the rug sits a small table complete with hors d'oeuvres, fresh strawberries and warm melted chocolate, all graced with more delicate rose petals— Valentine's Day at its finest!

Mesmerized by the flames reflected in each other's eyes, you kiss and share a toast.

"To us…"

All this and you never left home.

After a couple years of enjoying my creations, my husband realized it would be selfish to keep this all to ourselves. Why not share the love? What couple wouldn't get a kick out of these? It didn't take him long to persuade me the world needed a romantic resource, a place where couples could find help and inspiration to escape from so-so and ho-hum. So what began as an attempt to perk up our marriage, evolved into an opportunity to help others do the same.

> *"When you do the common things in life in an uncommon way you will command the attention of the world."*
>
> **GEORGE WASHINGTON CARVER**

This book is the first *and only* romantic entertaining and decorating book of its kind. It's not a cookbook. To the contrary, it's a how-to-cheat-and-eat-great book. It's not a how-to-have-great-sex book, but does give practical, back-to-basic principles of the little things that slip away over the years.

With each roomscape I have provided beautiful illustrations, simple checklists and step-by-step instructions. Use it to take your relationship from tired to energized, boring to adventurous and embers to flames.

As far back as I can remember, I have been a hopeless romantic. When I married Doug, I was certain I had found my Prince. He's thoughtful, affectionate and has a great sense of humor—all rolled up into tall, dark and handsome. I don't know how I got so lucky, but one thing I do know: luck will not sustain a marriage. Not for long anyway. Once the honeymoon began to wane, I came to the rude awakening it was going to take work to keep things interesting. To keep him wondering, "What'll she do next?" To keep him convinced the grass is greener on *this* side of the fence.

Who said you can't have an affair with your spouse?

"We've got this gift of love, but love is like a precious plant. You can't just accept it and leave it in the cupboard or just think it's going to get on by itself. You've got to keep watering it. You've got to really look after it and nurture it."

JOHN LENNON

We were both very young when we got married and I was eager to be a good little wife and do all the things good little wives do. So when our first few special occasions came around, I got busy. You know the drill—plan a menu, buy sexy lingerie, cook all day, light candles, turn on soft music… Ahhh, romantic bliss! And we lived happily ever after…

Well, not exactly. One by one those enchanted evenings didn't seem so enchanting anymore. To tell you the truth, they began to take on a strong resemblance to worn-out reruns. I searched high and low for fresh ideas, but came up empty-handed every time.

Then it hit me. I've always had a passion for themed, over-the-top parties; why not throw a party for two?

I began to implement the same props, décor and lighting I used in my large parties into small intimate settings and the results were stunning. Doug was ecstatic and I was hooked. As soon as one was over, I found myself anticipating and looking for inspiration for the next.

It's All About The Mood, Not About The Food

A couple of years later, an unexpected thing happened. Doug decided to reciprocate and host a Valentine's Day dinner for me. I was tickled, but skeptical. My husband is a great guy, but he does **not** cook. What would he serve—Beanie Weenies by candlelight? I hate to admit it, but my expectations were pretty low, but he blew them completely out of the water. He served an incredible meal consisting of a colorful crisp salad, juicy prime rib, sautéed mushrooms and twice baked potatoes. The grand finale: decadent turtle cheesecake.

Then he let me in on his secret. Almost the entire meal was made with prepared or precooked foods from the store. *You've got to be kidding. You mean all these years I've been wearing myself out cooking all day for nothing?*

This changed everything. Who's the genius that said a romantic dinner had to be made from scratch? For that matter, who said you had to cook at all? From then on, my motto became *"it's all about the mood, not about the food."*

I'm sure all the cooking aficionados are gasping in horror right now, but most of you are breathing a sigh of relief. Now, I'll liberate you even more. Burn your romantic cookbooks and find a great take-out menu.

I began mixing and matching combinations of take-out, prepared foods and simple make-ahead recipes and, "Voila!" mouth-watering meals with little or no cooking.

This new concept piqued my curiosity. I began mixing and matching combinations of take-out, prepared foods and simple make-ahead recipes and, "*Voila!*" mouth-watering meals with little or no cooking. Now you can enjoy the best of both worlds: delicious and intimate dinners in the privacy of your own home without cooking or guilt. How great is that?

Here's a sample of what I do most. A day or two in advance, I prepare a dessert; on the day of my dinner, I order an appetizer and entrée from a restaurant and at the last minute, I throw a simple salad together. It's up to you. Cook as much or as little as you want.

"Being over-scheduled is the biggest killer of romance because when we're tired and frazzled, we have nothing left for each other."

D.P. WASHINGTON

Now That's
Romantic!

Let's Get Started

MAKE A PLAN

Over the past thirty-plus years I have done the dinner thing dozens of times—some small simple ones, some big all-out productions and everything in-between. But I didn't do it without making mistakes of all shapes and sizes. I learned the best strategy to a successful evening is this:

> *Prepare anything and everything possible ahead of time.*
> *Do not wing it at the last minute.*

No matter how well you plan—inevitably something will sneak up on you, veer you off course and gobble up more time than you anticipated. You can count on it. The florist will lose your order or your babysitter will leave you stranded. Making the better part of your arrangements in advance will give you the time and flexibility to cope with last-minute predicaments. Sometimes that's the only cushion you have between a mess and a success.

> *"An ounce of prevention is worth a pound of cure."*
> **BENJAMIN FRANKLIN**

Ladies

Before getting dressed for the evening, schedule time to relax and unwind. Take a nap, a bubble bath, lie in the sun or get a massage. Stress and fatigue wreak havoc on our desire and libido; so pace yourself or you'll be too tired to tango.

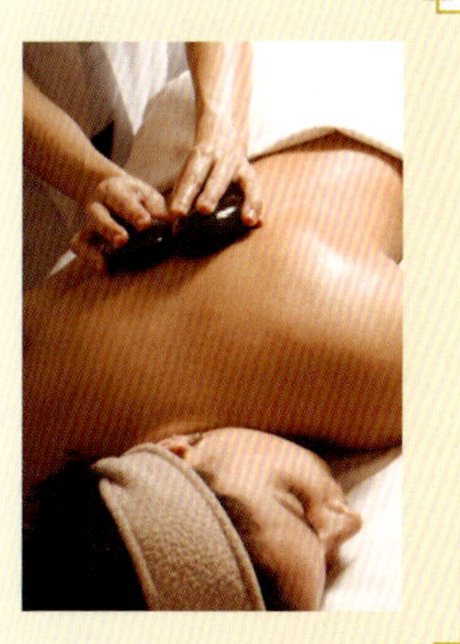

SURPRISE!

Anyone can make a reservation: that's the easy thing to do, it's also the *ordinary* thing to do. Let's face it, there's nothing exciting about *giving* an ordinary gift, and there's nothing exciting about *receiving* one either.

That's why I love surprises! And if you can't tell by now, I look for reasons and excuses to have fun and party. Not only do I want my victim to be surprised, I want it to be bigger and better than they ever imagined.

> *"It is more blessed to give than to receive."*
>
> ACTS 20:35 (NIV)

Have you ever found the perfect gift for a loved one, and knew they were going to love it so much you could hardly wait to give it? That's how I feel every time I conjure up a new roomscape. I get that giddy-as-a-schoolgirl, can't-wait-for-it-to-get-here attitude.

To let a special day slip by without commemorating it in one way or another is a wasted opportunity. On the other hand, there's no rule that says you have to wait for a special occasion. *Just because* can be the best reason of all.

Here are a few different ways to pull off your surprise. Choose the one that suits you and your situation best.

INVITATION ONLY

Whether store bought, handwritten or computer generated, a playful and steamy invitation will set the stage for your evening. When writing your invitation, don't give them any information other than the date, time and *maybe* what you want them to wear—but only if it doesn't spoil your surprise. Leave them in suspense for the rest.

For joint special occasions like anniversaries and Valentine's Day, avoid a possible conflict by giving them an invitation far in advance. *Never* assume your spouse isn't planning a surprise for you.

SEMI-SURPRISE

This one's my favorite. It's easy to pull off and creates an exhilarating air of anticipation. Here's how it works.

On the day of your big date, call, text or email your spouse and inform them you have schemed something up for the two of you that evening. Reveal *just enough* information to get their cooperation. It is important they understand exactly what time to arrive; a couple minutes late is okay, but it is absolutely, positively *not* okay to be early.

If your party is scheduled on a day your spouse is usually hanging around the house, give them a day or two notice. Ask them to make plans to get out of the house for however long it will take you to set up. Believe me, they'll be happy to oblige you.

When using the Semi-Invitation or Invitation Only Surprise, if possible, ask them to arrive dressed and date ready. Maybe they can use the gym locker room, your neighborhood clubhouse or a friend or relative's house. If not, have their clothes prepared and laid out for them when they arrive.

If you ordered take-out for dinner, ask them to pick it up on their way home. Use the time while they're getting dressed to plate appetizers and organize or warm up food.

A customer, I'll call Lisa, hired me to assist her for their anniversary. She chose the Secluded Safari and she wanted it to be an all weekend event. She also wanted to carry the theme from the master bedroom into the living room. But that posed a problem. Her husband would need a shower when he got home and that meant he would have to pass through the master bedroom to get to the master bathroom, and she didn't want him to see the bedroom until later in the evening.

She decided she would greet him at the door, hand him a bamboo basket filled with his favorite toiletries and a new pair of boxer shorts then detour him to the guest bathroom.

Here's how her plan actually unfolded. He walked in, got one glimpse of Lisa in her hot leopard lingerie standing in the midst of the candlelight…

He never made it to the guest bath.

The entire operation is kept undercover until they walk through the door. This is more challenging and should be handled exactly as you would a typical surprise party. Recruit a co-conspirator or a dependable friend or relative who can keep a secret and who can come up with a strategy to keep your guest of honor occupied and out of your way until party time.

If your spouse travels, plan your surprise upon their return.

Do Not Disturb

Parents, how many of you have experienced this mood-shattering scenario? The kids are asleep, you're finally alone, caught up in an intimate moment and oblivious to the world around you. Then…wide-eyed, silent and standing at the foot of your bed is your innocent little darling.

Scrambling for the sheets, you gasp, "Sweetie! How long have you been standing there?"

Kids and romance do not mix. All couples need time alone, *really* alone. If you have family or friends willing to baby-sit your little angels, allow them the privilege. If you can finagle overnight or weekend accommodations, that's even better. Treat yourselves to the luxury of waking up at your leisure, lounging in your underwear and lingering over coffee.

That goes ditto for Fido; if he's underfoot and shadowing your every move, get a sitter for him too.

TEENAGERS

They're old enough to know what goes on behind *closed doors,* but don't think twice about *knocking* on closed doors. They're notorious for popping in and out of the house with little or no warning, frequently with friends in tow. The best way to deal with teens is to just come right out and say it: "*We want to be A-L-O-N-E.*" They'll get over it.

Rule #1: **Go away.** Have them plan a sleepover with a friend. Confirm the arrangements with the friend's parents and if you're comfortable, tell the parents about your special occasion and offer to return the favor for them someday.

Rule #2: **No excuses.** Before they leave the house, make sure there is no reason to call or come back home. Pack everything they could possibly need or want. Toothbrush, bed roll, P.J.s, bathing suit, money, retainer, iPOD, CDs, DVDs, video games, controllers, snacks, etc.

Rule #3: **No misunderstandings.** Give them written instructions. Detail what they are and are not allowed to do, where they can or can't go and who they can or can't do it with. Don't forget curfews. If it's not written down, it's "NO." If it will prevent confusion, give a copy to their friend's parents as well.

Rule #4: **Stay Away.** Issue strict orders that home is forbidden territory and if they don't heed your warning, there will be swift and labor-intensive consequences.

It's amazing how liberating it is to have the run of your *own* home. Privacy, peace and quiet, neat and orderly… You may be tempted to change the locks.

Turn OFF the TV.

Turn OFF the telephone.

Turn ON each other.

Helpful Hint

If you decide to leave your cell phone on, program it with your babysitter's or teen's personal tune or ringtone. Better yet, block all calls except theirs.

CLEAN YOUR ROOM

Have you ever read one of those labels on a blow dryer that said **"WARNING: Do not operate while bathing?"** They wouldn't have put it there unless somebody had actually tried it. That's how I feel about this topic.

WARNING: Do not attempt to create a romantic atmosphere in a dirty, messy space. Clutter, dirty dishes and smelly laundry will short-circuit any fantasy you attempt to create. The two cannot co-exist. You cannot escape reality if it's peeking over your shoulder all night.

If you're allergic to cleaning, at the very least, stuff the clutter in a box and hide it in a closet or another room. A little dusting and a little vacuuming should do it. It doesn't have to be white-glove perfect, but it should look orderly and attractive by candlelight. This is a must for every room or space you'll be using.

Your table setting should not only be attractive, it should instigate lots of smooching and eye contact. If your table is small enough to face each other, hold hands and play footsies, that's perfect. But if it's large, cozy up next to each other on a corner. Be sure to remove all table leaves.

To prevent unwelcome last-minute surprises (the kind of surprises I don't like) a week or two before your dinner, set up your entire table setting for a sneak preview. If possible, set up when it's dark so you can evaluate your lighting and candle needs.

- Tablecloth (Iron, if necessary.)
- Plates, salad plates, bowls
- Placemats or chargers
- Glassware: water glasses, wine, champagne or cocktail glasses
- Napkins (Ironed, folded or in their napkin rings.)
- Flatware
- Candleholders
- Candles
- Low watt or flicker-flame light bulbs for chandelier, if needed
- Vase *without* fresh flowers

How does it look? Does it need tweaking? If so, make your adjustments. If you like what you see, pack the whole thing in a box and stash it away until showtime. Your table setting will practically appear out of nowhere.

Not sure which side the forks goes on? See the photo above or download and print at *nowthatsromantic.com*.

LIGHTING

Lighting is the easiest and most affordable way to add drama to a room. It breathes life and character into a space and is the most essential element of any intimate setting. It doesn't matter how much time, money or effort you put into your roomscape, without proper lighting, it's all for nothing.

Here are a few techniques to whet your imagination.

Up Lights Up lights are easy to find, inexpensive and a cinch to use. Place them behind a screen, under a tree, or a cluster of branches. Plug them in and flip the switch. "Presto!" Shadows are splattered across walls and ceilings, instantly transforming a humdrum room into one bursting with intrigue. Use 25 or 40 watt bulbs in up lights.

White Christmas Lights White Christmas lights are versatile and enchanting. Nestle them in trees and greenery or wrap them around columns and handrails on porches and balconies.

Always try to match the color of the wire to its surroundings: green or brown wire for plants and trees and white wire for white columns and handrails.

Leave the lights in your greenery year round. When they're off, they're invisible—when they're on, instant ambiance and sparkle.

Never use up lights and Christmas lights at the same time. They conflict with each another.

Dimmer Switches Soften the light of chandeliers and sconces with dimmer switches or low watt bulbs. Before you head to the store, be sure to check the size of your sockets. Are they large or small? Depending on your theme, flicker-flame bulbs can provide a nice alternative.

Let me be clear. I'm *not* talking about putting dimmer switches on overhead lighting. Overhead lighting should never be used in a romantic setting. It will wash out all the special effects you've worked so hard to create.

Likewise, overhead kitchen lights are a glaring and harsh intruder if they spill into your entertaining space. Turn them off and illuminate your countertops with under cabinet lighting, nightlights or candles.

Candlelight A romantic dinner without candlelight is… well… impossible. Candles are *essential*. They make any occasion feel festive and their soft flickering glow is *intoxicating*.

Let's face it, the darker it is, the more attractive we become.

Candles come in a never-ending variety of colors and fragrances, which can make shopping for them a perplexing task. Relax. It's not as complicated as you might think. Before you head to the store, keep these basic guidelines in mind.

> *"When the candles are out all women are fair."*
>
> **PLUTARCH**

Strong, perfumey fragrances—especially when using several candles at a time—can be suffocating. When mixed with the aroma of food, it can be downright nauseating. I want you to take their breath away, but scrambling for their inhaler is not what I had in mind. While dining, burn only unscented or mildly scented candles.

I know, I know, I can hear you complaining already. "But I love all those exotic fragrances." I do too. And you can still use them—only *after* dinner.

When choosing a fragrance, stay consistent with your theme. Scents like lime, mango or pineapple complement the Caribbean Cabana, while rose, strawberry and cashmere add to the Hearts on Fire experience.

Choosing color is even simpler: white or off-white. When lit, the entire body of the candle *glows* and when used in abundance, they cast an ethereal spell.

You may be thinking, "But what if I want a lime scented candle? They're always green. Or strawberry? They're red or pink."

That's an easy fix. Use unscented white candles for your décor, but tart warmers with scented wax tarts, cubes or chips for your fragrance. The varieties are endless and they won't interfere with your color scheme.

Safety First

ALWAYS *practice safety when placing candles, especially near fabrics. Battery operated candles are a safe alternative and can be used anywhere a live flame could pose a hazard.*

NEVER *leave a candle unattended.*

ALWAYS *keep a fire extinguisher in a handy, inconspicuous location.*

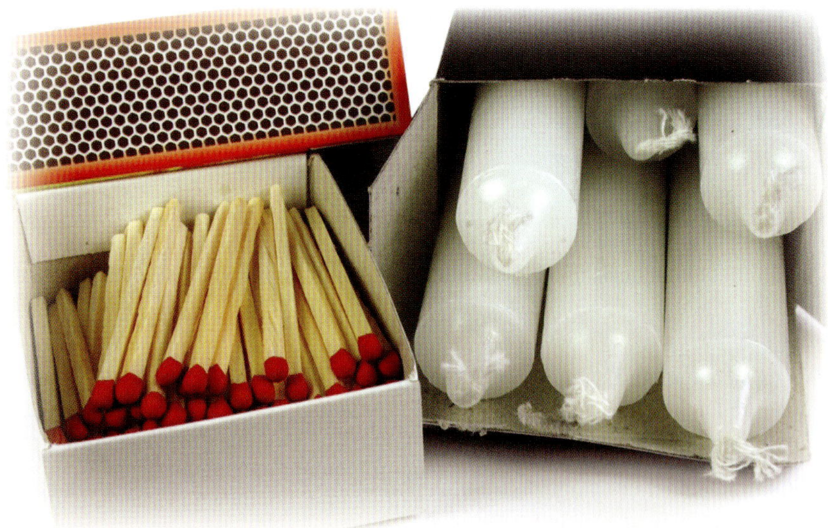

Now That's
Romantic!

MUSIC

Music is the universal language of the soul—an audible flame that can melt hearts and spark passion. In an instant, we can visit the past and relive all the emotions and sensations of that moment. Music is potent and powerful. Use with caution.

Play Lists Creating a play list gives you the flexibility to choose the type and order of your music. With the help of the Internet, it only takes minutes to locate and download any song ever recorded. Play lists also make a wonderful keepsake.

CDs, iPODs, thumb drives and computers are all great for creating a play list, but an iPOD is discreet and its small glowing face is perfect for operating in the dark.

Specialty Music Compilations These are fabulous music collections of specialty genres and moods that are perfect for soft background music while dining. The varieties are endless: instrumental romance, piano, violin, steel drums, mariachi guitar, Zen, reggae, big band, nature sounds, 60's, 70's, 80's…. The list goes on and on and on. They are readily available online and on display in most department stores and gift shops.

Satellite Radio Satellite radio takes no thought or effort, but the deejay dialogue and commercials are rude interruptions from the outside world and the play list is beyond your control. You might get all hits. You might get all duds.

Cable Music Channels Cable music channels have no commercials or corny deejays, but the glare of

"Music expresses that which cannot be said and on which it is impossible to be silent."

VICTOR HUGO

the TV screen will spoil the effects of your candlelight and lighting. Like satellite radio, you are back to the luck of the draw on song choice.

Music Sets Consider breaking your music into two sets: A During Dinner Set and an After Dinner Set. The During Dinner Set should be light, relaxing and conducive for conversation. Two hours of music should be sufficient.

Your After Dinner Set should coincide with your after dinner activities. If you want to heat things up a bit, choose dance, sexy or erotic tunes. Plan for more music than you think you'll need, at least two to three hours. Just remember, it can be very anti-climactic if the music ends before you do.

When planning your music, stick with your theme. For instance, pair Christmas love songs with the Santa Baby roomscape or African wildlife blended with musical rhythms with The Secluded Safari.

AFTER DINNER ACTIVITIES

Great parties always have something to do besides eat. So plan a provocative after dinner activity. For example: with the Hearts on Fire roomscape, finger-paint with your chocolate fondue; with the Caribbean Cabana, if you have a pool or hot tub, go skinny-dipping; and with Surrender the Booty, give it up for a lap dance or striptease.

For Lovers

Fall in Love Again and Again and Again…

Over the years—one seemingly insignificant gesture at a time—we became lax in *doing* the things lovers do. Consequently, we ceased *being* lovers. The solution is simple. Reverse the process.

"Though no one can go back and make a brand new start, anyone can start from now and make a brand new ending."

CARL BARD

Get back to the basics. When was the last time you…

…kissed, not a mindless peck hello or goodbye, but a warm, lingering smooch?

"'Twas not my lips you kissed but my soul."

JUDY GARLAND

…talked, not just exchanged a few words, but a pleasant fifteen minute conversation?

…held hands, walking in the mall or riding in the car?

…cuddled, watching a movie or before you got out of bed in the morning?

…laughed together?

…called for no reason except to say, "I love you, I'm thinking about you?"

> "I like not only to be loved, but to be
> told I am loved."
>
> **GEORGE ELIOT**

…noticed something praiseworthy—then gave a sincere compliment?

> "I can live for two months on a good compliment."
>
> **MARK TWAIN**

…flirted, winked, pinched or teased each other?

Start doing the things lovers do, and before you know it, you will be.

> "A successful marriage requires falling in love many
> times, always with the same person."
>
> **MIGNON MCLAUGHLIN**

SPICE IT UP

Our bodies require a variety of foods to keep us nourished and our love lives are no different. They too need variety to thrive. Most of us would go crazy if we ate the same thing day after day, week after week. Torturing our libido with bland monotony is no different. So, spice it up.

30

For Ladies Only

Dress For Success

The phrase "dress for success," is a widely used axiom in the business world, but the principle is every bit as true for a successful marriage. Without saying a word, our appearance speaks volumes. What do your clothes say about you? What do they say to your husband? Do you wear granny drawers and frumpy flannel and then wonder why you don't *feel* amorous or desirable?

"When I undress a woman, and notice that she is wearing ugly underwear, it makes me feel three things: One, that she must not care that much about herself if she can actually wear that stuff; two, that she must not care that much about me to let me see her wearing that stuff; and three, that she must not care that much about sex, because she couldn't possibly feel sexy wearing that stuff!"

GREGORY J.P. GODEK
1001 MORE WAYS TO BE ROMANTIC

Practice being sexy. You heard me right. I said *practice*. When you put on something sexy, how do you feel? Awkward? Uncomfortable? You, my dear, are out of practice.

Take inventory—from the top of your head to the tips of your toes. Bring your hairstyle and make-up into the 21st century. Lose weight. Get a little sun. Treat your tootsies to a pedicure. No excuses. If drag queens can dress up like women and be drop-dead gorgeous, so can you.

Staging Your Comeback, The Makeover Guy by Christopher Hopkins is a fun and excellent read. It's loaded with unbelievable makeovers and gives simple, practical tips and techniques on how to take *your* body type and *your* personality and transform it from "dowdy to dazzling." The book is targeted to women over 45, but the concepts apply to any age.

Don't misunderstand me. I'm not trying to turn you into a Stepford Wife, but I am trying to encourage you to live up to your potential and be the most attractive wife and lover possible. After all, he chose *you* and you are the only one he's got.

You may be saying, "But Kim, my husband loves me just the way I am. He doesn't need all that."

Wait a minute. Do you realize how lucky you are? He loves you unconditionally—warts and all. That kind of love deserves to be rewarded, not taken for granted. He may not need it, but he wants it.

I hope my husband never feels he's missing out on any good thing because he picked me. And we all know men rate sex and an attractive wife near the top of their "good things" list.

32

THE ART OF SEDUCTION

Whether we admit it or not, we all long to be desired. This is especially true for men. They fantasize about you, their lover, so overcome by desire you will abandon your ladylike inhibitions and have your way with him. Why is this so hard? We're terrified, that's why.

"Okay Kim, let's say I put on a teddy and a pair of stilettos. Then what? I'll feel like a monkey in a suit. I won't know how to act or what to do. I'll feel awkward…. self-conscious… Oh forget it! I've changed my mind already."

Out of sheer intimidation, you just talked yourself out of the whole thing. The problem is, we own the equipment; we just don't know how, or we've forgotten how, to use it.

This brings me to my next point…

LEARN FROM THE PROS

Before you freak out, hear me out. One of the best ways I have found to get the equipment up and running is dance. There are instructional Latin dance, erotic dance and striptease videos presented in wholesome ways that can teach you how to feel confident in your own skin. The slow fluid moves

"Her husband has full confidence in her and lacks nothing of value."

PROVERBS 31:11 (NIV)

will not only allow you to embrace your femininity, you will feel graceful and beautiful doing them. The experience and know-how of strip and lap dancing will equip you with prowess you didn't know you had. It's a great workout and an empowering spring of sensuality. I can't recommend it enough.

Actress Sheila Kelley, while preparing for a movie role as a stripper, began studying in local strip clubs. In her book *The S Factor, Strip Workouts for Every Woman*, she was amazed that in the midst of such a sordid and depraved atmosphere how graceful and captivating the women's movements were. It changed her life, her body and her marriage.

If making your husband weak with desire is a skill you would like to acquire, her book and DVDs will help you do just that. They are tastefully designed and created for women only.

Other DVDs are also available in department stores and online. Do them in the privacy of your home or join a gym or dance studio. Even if you never work up the nerve to actually dance or strip for your husband, do it for yourself. You will be amazed at how many moves and techniques you will actually take into your bedroom.

"But Kim, strippers are sleazy. I could never do that."

Think of it this way. It's not *what* she's doing, it's *whom* she's doing it for and the fact she's doing it for *money* that's sleazy. But one thing we can agree on, she is a master at the art of pleasing a man, and if you can learn something from her to please *your* man—Why not? Beat them at their own game.

You may be wondering, "This woman claims to be a Christian. How can she recommend this stuff?"

If you think God is a prude, think again. If you want to know what the creator of sex and marriage thinks about the subject, I suggest the book *Intimacy Ignited, Fire Up Your Sex Life with the Song of Solomon* by Dr. Joseph & Linda Dillow and Dr. Peter & Lorraine Pintus. It is a verse-by-verse translation of the Song of Songs, the poetic and symbolic book in the Bible that depicts the hot and steamy love life of King Solomon and his wife. *Yes, there's even erotic dancing!*

Now back to our dinners.

DRESSING THE PART

When choosing what to wear for your special occasion, there are two hard and fast rules:

Rule #1:

*It must be something that makes **you** feel irresistible.*

and

Rule #2:

*It must be something that will make **him** crazy with desire.*

It should turn *both* of you on.

One of the perks of these parties is you can dress as risqué as you dare. Don't get hung up on lingerie. Nightclub wear, resort wear or a costume can be even better.

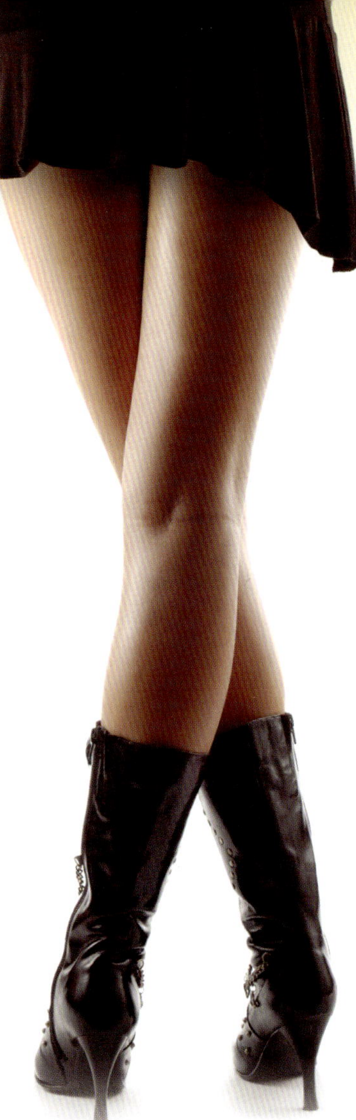

ACCENT YOUR ASSETS

Before you hit the mall, have a plan. What's your best feature? Are you blessed with voluptuous breasts? Show them off with a plunging neckline. Do you have an hourglass waist? Accentuate it with an open midriff. Long, slender legs? Flaunt them with a micro-mini and stilettos. When we make our assets the focal point, we divert attention away from our imperfections.

Become proficient at provocative dress. At every turn, Hollywood is inundating us with sex appeal: billboards, television, magazines and music videos. Use it to your advantage—to your husband's advantage. Watch and learn. Some of the sexiest outfits I've ever seen were *not* in lingerie shops.

You don't have to buy something new or spend a lot of money. Browse through your closet with a seductress' eye. Convert ordinary clothing into hot and racy items by skipping *proper* undergarments or leaving buttons *inadvertently* undone. I have landed some saucy little cocktail dresses at consignment shops—some with the tags still attached. I have also made some of my outfits for next to nothing.

Here I go again, sounding like a broken record, but when planning what to wear, *stick with your theme*. For instance, if you are hosting The Secluded Safari, think Tarzan and Jane, Warrior Woman, wild and primitive, leather or leopard skins. Add beads or bone jewelry,

arm cuff bracelets, bronze skin lotion, feathered hair extensions, tousled hair and exotic eye make-up.

Pay attention to the details. Change your hairstyle with a wig, streak or extensions. Try shimmering or sparkling body lotions, eyelashes, nail polish, hair accessories, hosiery and footwear. Embellish your lower back with a large temporary tattoo or place a small one in a strategic spot for an extra element of surprise. The possibilities are endless. Get into *character*. Don't be surprised if it turns *you* on as much as it does him.

Finally, the most crucial element: skin. Bare, soft, delicious skin. Make your body irresistibly touchable with a luxurious soak and a gentle exfoliator. Silky, shaved flesh is a must. And for a dewy, radiant glow, apply a sheer layer of body lotion containing mica.

While still in the buff, lightly dab or mist perfume all over. Before you dress, lightly mist your clothing. The key word here is *lightly*, you don't want to be a room freshener; the goal is to be *delicately* scented from head to toe. No matter where he nuzzles, he should want to draw closer and breathe you in.

So what are you waiting for? Wake the ravishing creature inside you. Stretch your limits. Make one improvement. That improvement will spark another and another. Success breeds success. Before you know it, you'll love the woman looking at you in the mirror, and that ignites confidence. **And confidence is sexy!**

> *"Confidence is the sexiest thing a woman can have. It's much sexier than any body part."*
>
> **AIMEE MULLINS**

For Men Only

Romance 101

No one will argue the fact that men and women have obvious physical differences. But here's where it gets tricky. Men and women have emotional and psychological differences too, but these differences are obscure and hard to define.

What I'm trying to say is this: men are wired and turned on through their eyes, while women are wooed through their minds and hearts. *Bottom line—sex is a major priority to men while romance is equally, if not more important, to women.*

> "Women are meant to be loved, not understood."
>
> **OSCAR WILDE**

You are probably asking yourself, "If our instinctive traits are at such odds, how can any marriage survive?"

It's not easy, but with patience and understanding, these differences can be learned and respected. When that happens, each complements the other, and without the other, each is incomplete. Like Yin and Yang and a lock and key—these polarizing characteristics will actually work together to balance and strengthen the relationship, not tear it down.

So what is romance? Romance is when words are unable to express your feelings and actions must fill the gap. It doesn't just say "I love you," it *demonstrates* it.

Romance is doing the little extras she doesn't need —but desperately wants. It can be a simple walk in the park, writing "I Love You" on a steamy bathroom mirror or calling just to say, "I'm thinking about you." It's also relieving her of a dreaded chore or giving her a break from the kids to bask in a leisurely bubble bath or lunch with a friend. The very core of romance is putting her wants above your own. It makes her feel special and beautiful—it puts a smile on her face and a song in her heart.

In most homes, wives have the daily responsibilities of cooking, cleaning, grocery shopping and laundry… the unending demand of meeting everyone else's needs. So it speaks volumes when a husband goes out of his way to plan custom-made time for the two of you. Time that has been thought out and every detail anticipated. Time for her to sit back, relax and not worry about a thing—it screams, "He loves me. He appreciates me. He did this all for me!"

You may be thinking, "That sounds like a lot of work. I already do all the things husbands are supposed to do. I bring her roses and chocolates on Valentine's Day and a card and gift on her birthday and Christmas. I tell her I love her."

That's great. And you should do those things. But what romance is not, is sliding into cookie-cutter mode. In other words, she doesn't want to be another *thing* you check off your "to-do" list. You don't want sex like that and she doesn't want romance like that either.

The same holds true when you say, "I love you." You can say it every time you hang up the phone and every night when you turn off the lights, but nothing says "I love you" like your actions.

Romance doesn't rush. It's patient and lingers in the moment. Holding, kissing, caressing… It doesn't hurry to get to the good parts.

> *"Let's not merely say that we love each other; let us show the truth by our actions."*
>
> **1 JOHN 3:18 (NLT)**

PAY IT FORWARD

"Okay Kim, I get it. Women *need* romance. But what about my needs?"

Women are not the great mystery men make them out to be. They're profoundly simple. In a nutshell, women don't want to be intimate if they don't *feel* loved. So pay it forward. If you want sex, give her romance. A natural by-product of tender romance is passionate sex and the best sex isn't what happens in bed, but what leads up to it. Don't be surprised if she is so grateful, she starts going out of her way to please you in return.

CHIVALRY NEVER GOES OUT OF STYLE

Women admire and esteem a true gentleman. I'm not talking about snobby etiquette. I'm talking about a man who is polite, gracious and mannerly—a virtue that radiates from the inside out. It's one of the most irresistible traits a man can possess.

I think I speak for the majority of the female population when I say *I love being treated like a lady.* I am perfectly capable of opening doors or handling my chair, but these old-fashioned acts of kindness have become a rare commodity. Manners and common courtesy have fallen by the wayside and gentlemen are becoming a dying breed. Gone are the days when men wouldn't dream of being rude or profane in a woman's presence.

Chivalry may be a lost art, but it will **never** go out of style.

A SHARP-DRESSED MAN

Packaging is everything. It doesn't matter if you work on Wall Street and wear a three-piece suit or live on a ranch and wear Levis. A well-groomed, well-dressed man is not only sexy, he commands confidence and respect before he utters a word.

Image matters. Women like eye candy too.

I can hear you guys already, "What do you mean women like eye candy? You just said women are not visually *turned on* the way men are."

True. But women are visually *turned off.* The Neanderthal look won't cut it. That's why cavemen used clubs and had to drag their mates by the hair to have sex with them.

So if you don't own a full-length mirror, get one. Then use it. Now pretend you're dating again. Are you a catch? If the answer is "No," you've got work to do.

Start by finding a hairstyle, not just a haircut. You might be wearing the latest trend, but that doesn't mean it looks good on you. Find an up-to-date style that works for you—your face, your build, your age and your personality.

Now get out the trimmers. Facial hair should be neat and trimmed, that includes your neck, nose and ears. And please, no scraggly uni-brows.

Brush and floss those pearly whites. By the way, are they still white? Nowadays, whitening your teeth is an easy and inexpensive fix; teeth-whitening kits can be purchased in any supermarket or drug store.

JAMES BROWN

Now let's talk wardrobe. Do your clothes match? Are they in good condition? Are you stuck in a time warp? Do you wear them wrinkled out of the dryer? Need I mention they *must* be clean?

It's easy to find the latest looks and fashions. You can learn a lot from magazines and department store advertisements. Notice how they match prints with solids and shirts with pants. Find a style that complements your shape, age and personality. Remember, a proper fit is crucial.

How about that physique? Are you sporting a keg? Aside from the fact that being overweight is unhealthy, it's unattractive. Women don't like fat and flabby any more than men do. Get off the couch. Eat smart. Start an exercise regime. Walk. Join a gym. Get in shape.

Fingernails and toenails may seem like piddly details, but you can learn a lot about someone by the way they care for their hands and feet. Unkempt nails convey you probably handle other areas of your life in a similar manner. Long, dirty toenails are disturbing, especially in light of the fact that nail clippers are cheap, easy to use and it only takes minutes to keep them in respectable condition.

If you aren't sure where to start, invest in a manicure and pedicure. Watch how the professionals do it. Men's nails don't need to be perfect and polished, but they must be clean, trimmed and the rough edges filed smooth.

Have you ever noticed how women open and sniff *everything?* Lotions, air fresheners, candles… We're obsessed with scents. If we're so concerned about how the laundry smells, don't you think we want our man to smell great too? If you don't have a masculine scent of your own, it's time to find one.

Three-tenths of good looks are due to nature; seven-tenths to dress."

PROVERB

Just in case you're toying with the notion of strutting your stuff in some itsy-bitsy man thong because you think it will turn her on, ask yourself this question first. Why are there so many lingerie shops for women but none for men? It goes full circle to what I said at the beginning of this chapter about women not being visually turned on the way men are. Male lingerie could prove embarrassing, and chances are it won't do a thing for her libido. So when it comes to romance, it's best to play it safe and err on the side of class and sophistication.

Let The Show Begin

Each roomscape is loaded with ideas. Please, please, please *do not feel you have to do them all.* Some may work in your home while others may not. Customize and adapt them to suit you and your home. Make them intimately yours by infusing your own personal touches. Feel free to improvise with similar items you already have. You don't have to do it exactly by the book. They won't miss what they never saw. They'll love it just the same and that's what really counts.

Each roomscape is divided into four categories: Table Setting, Décor & Lighting, Sounds & Scents and What to Wear. Each one also has a Things You'll Need checklist to help you stay organized. In the back of the book I have provided a Time Line to keep you on schedule. Photocopy it, or download and print it at *nowthatsromantic.com.*

The Caribbean Cabana

Drift away to the crystal azure waters of the Caribbean… Feel the balmy breezes caress your skin as they whisper through palm trees and the white linens of your cabana… Let the easy-going rhythm of steel drums melt your worries… Delicate orchids adorn your table while you savor an icy Margarita and succulent crab cakes.

This is where it all began. My very first roomscape.

Our anniversary falls in April, and in Florida, the weather is perfect—warm sunny days, cool comfortable nights, low humidity and no mosquitoes. By this time, without fail, Doug and I are both suffering from a severe case of *beach fever*. That particular year, the odds of getting relief on a sandy seashore were nil. So I did the next best thing, I brought the islands to us.

Maybe you're in a similar situation and taking a vacation isn't a doable option. No problem *mon*. Take a staycation instead. All you need is a porch, patio or balcony. If you own a pool or live near the water, that's even better.

Dine on tropical fare as you watch the sun set, then let the sound of the waves lull you to sleep.

Can you feel your latitude changing?

- [ ] 2 yards aqua fabric or tablecloth
- [ ] 2 sets of white dishes and salad bowls
- [ ] 2 large scallop shells or shell-shaped appetizer plates, optional
- [ ] 2 white tortoise shell chargers
- [ ] 2 sets of flatware
- [ ] 2 Margarita glasses
- [ ] 2 white or off-white napkins
- [ ] 1 4-inch ivory pillar candle
- [ ] 1 tall hurricane lantern
- [ ] 3 clear votive candleholders, optional
- [ ] 3 white votive candles, optional
- [ ] White beach sand or shell filler
- [ ] 5 small colorful seashells
- [ ] Raffia
- [ ] 4-5 dozen large white orchid blossoms
- [ ] 2 or more real or silk palms trees
- [ ] 84 or 96-inch white cotton panels or white muslin/ duck cloth (See How to Calculate Panel Fabric Yardage page 54.)
- [ ] Small nails, staple gun or drapery hardware, if desired
- [ ] White cotton cording/ribbon (See How to Calculate Tieback Yardage page 54.)
- [ ] Command Strips™, optional
- [ ] Queen/double mattress or air or futon mattress
- [ ] 2-4 pillows
- [ ] Tan queen/double sheet set, with 2-4 pillowcases
- [ ] Round mosquito net kit
- [ ] 1 eyehook
- [ ] White chain (1-3 feet) length depends on your ceiling height
- [ ] 2 up lights, optional
- [ ] Tart warmer, optional
- [ ] Scented tart, cube or wax chips, optional

Caribbean
Cabana

- Drape the aqua fabric or tablecloth on the patio table.

- Set each place with chargers, dishes, scallop shells, flatware, napkins and glassware.

- Pour 2-3 inches of beach sand or shell filler in the hurricane lantern.

- Center the pillar candle in the hurricane lantern.

- Arrange the small seashells around the pillar candle.

- Tie raffia around the base of the hurricane lantern.

- Place the hurricane lantern on the table.

- Place the votive candles on the table, optional.

- Scatter orchids on the table.

DÉCOR & LIGHTING

- Hang the white panels or fabric with the small nails, staple gun or drapery hardware.

- To make the tiebacks, cut the cording/ribbon into 24-inch strips. Tie knots on the ends to prevent fraying.

- Using nails, staples or Command Strips™ attach the tiebacks to your walls, poles, screen frame, etc.

- Determine the location for your mattress and install the eyehook into the ceiling centered above that location.

- Hang the white chain from the eyehook.

- Attach the mosquito net to the white chain. The net should drag the floor by approximately 24-inches.

- While propping or holding the net to the side, place the mattress directly under the mosquito net.

- Put the sheets and pillows on the mattress.

- Drape the mosquito net evenly around the head and sides of the mattress.

- Place your palm trees.

- Place the up lights under and behind the palm trees, optional.

- Scatter the orchid blossoms on the bed overflowing onto the surrounding floor.

Caribbean
Cabana

If you have neighbors in close proximity, wider or more panels may be required. When or if more privacy is needed, unfasten the tiebacks and allow the panels to close. Plants and palm trees can also be strategically positioned to obstruct the view of unwelcome spectators.

HOW TO CALCULATE PANEL FABRIC AND TIEBACK YARDAGE

PANELS

First decide how many panels you're going to need. Next, determine (in inches) the length you want to make your panels. Then, multiply the number of panels by the length. Then divide that number by 36 inches to get your yardage.

Example:

Number of panels = 8. Length = 96 inches. 8 panels x 96 inches = 768 inches. Divide 768 inches by 36 inches = 21.33 yards.

TIE BACKS

You will need 1 tieback per panel. Multiply that number by 24 inches. Then divide by 36 inches to determine yardage.

Example:

8 panels = 8 tiebacks. 8 tiebacks x 24 inches = 192 inches. Divide 192 inches by 36 inches = 5.33 yards

The first time I did this roomscape, I used unfinished fabric and attached it to the walls with thumbtacks. We loved the cool airiness of the panels so much, the following spring I bought ready-made cotton panels and hardware, hung them and left them up the entire summer. Now I can't imagine summer without them.

SOUNDS & SCENTS

Sounds:

During Dinner:
Ocean sounds: *The Calming Ocean* CD, Calypso: *Don't Stop the Carnival (Instrumental Carnival Hits)* CD, Steel Drum Island Collection: *Hot Hot Hot & More on Steel Drums* CD

After Dinner:
Jimmy Buffett's *Songs You Know by Heart* CD, Bob Marley's *Legend (Remastered)* CD, UB40's *Greatest Hits* CD

Scents:

Lime, Mango, Coconut

If you'd like to add some realistic sound effects, try using two music sources, one with rolling waves and seagull sounds in the background, the other playing island tunes in the foreground.

WHAT TO WEAR

Women:

- Bathing suit, bikini or t-back with a sarong

- Sexy tropical resort or cruise wear

- Soaking wet, white or pastel cami or tank top with bikini bottoms only, wet hair, waterproof mascara

Accessorize with an orchid or hibiscus in your hair, eyelashes, shell necklace and earrings, waist chain, anklet, toe ring, strappy sandals or bare feet, French pedicure, tan: real, lotion or spray-on.

Men:

- Tropical shirt and cargo shorts

- Tank top and swim trunks or board shorts

- Sandals, flip-flops or bare feet

56

Hearts On Fire

Colorful rose petals beckon the way to a room brimming with flickering firelight, the fragrance of roses and the sounds of tender love songs. But that's just the beginning. The trail leads on and encircles a velvety white heart-shaped bearskin rug lying in the warm radiance of a brilliant fire. Beside the rug sits a small table complete with hors d'oeuvres, fresh strawberries and warm melted chocolate, all graced with more delicate rose petals—Valentine's Day at its finest!

Mesmerized by the flames reflected in each other's eyes, you kiss and share a toast.

"To us…"

 Valentine's Day bursting with ambiance, nothing heats things up quite like fire, fur and flowers. It's the essence of sensuousness—glowing firelight, passionate music, gooey chocolate, rose petals, rose petals and more rose petals and...*bare skin on bearskin.*

THINGS YOU'LL NEED

- [ ] 1½-2 yards pink satin or tablecloth
- [ ] 2 off-white salad/appetizer plates
- [ ] 2 forks
- [ ] 2 champagne flutes or martini glasses
- [ ] 2 off-white napkins
- [ ] 2 off-white serving pedestals or dinner plates and matching bowls
- [ ] 1 off-white serving or dinner plate
- [ ] 3 serving utensils, optional
- [ ] 2 off-white or clear candlestick holders
- [ ] 2 off-white taper candles for candlesticks
- [ ] Champagne bucket, optional
- [ ] Off-white vase with pink rose arrangement
- [ ] 5 off-white or clear votive or tea light candleholders
- [ ] 5 off-white votives or tea light candles
- [ ] 15-21 off-white pillar candles in various heights for the mantel and hearth
- [ ] 2 yards of white faux fur
- [ ] Firewood or artificial firewood i.e., Duraflame®
- [ ] Real or silk rose petals: white, light pink and dark pink
- [ ] Small fondue set
- [ ] 1 silk or live tree, optional
- [ ] 1 string of Christmas lights, 100 lights with green wire, optional
- [ ] 1 extension cord, if necessary
- [ ] Tart warmer, optional
- [ ] Scented tart, cube or wax chips, optional

TABLE SETTING

- Position the coffee table near the fireplace.

- Spread the pink satin fabric or tablecloth on the coffee table.

- Set the table with salad/appetizer plates, forks, napkins and glasses.

- Place the pink rose arrangement in the back middle of the table.

- Flank the candlesticks on each side of the rose arrangement.

- Position the serving plate in front of the rose arrangement and the serving pedestals on each side of the serving plate.

- Place the fondue pot on one side of the coffee table.

- Place the champagne bucket on the opposite side of the coffee table, optional.

- Arrange the votives or tea lights around the table.

- Sprinkle the rose petals evenly around the table.

For tips on how to make serving pedestals, go to ***nowthatsromantic.com***.

DÉCOR & LIGHTING

- Clean fireplace if necessary.

- Place the firewood in the fireplace.

- Nestle the Christmas lights in the tree.

- Arrange the pillar candles across the mantel and hearth.

- Cut the faux fur in the shape of a heart. (See How to Make Your Heart-Shaped Fur Rug, page 66.)

- Lay the fur rug in front of the hearth.

- Arrange your furniture around the rug and coffee table to envelope the space and create a feeling of intimacy.

- Position the tree with the Christmas lights in it and plug the lights in using the extension cord if necessary.

- Sprinkle a trail of rose petals from the doorway to the fur rug and around the rug.

Fireplace Alternatives

If you don't have a fireplace, your fireplace doesn't work, or if it's too warm for a fire, try one of these alternatives:

- Arrange several off-white pillar candles of various heights inside the fireplace.

- Purchase a fireplace candleholder. (See below.)

- Place a large framed mirror against the wall with the same candle arrangement mentioned above in front of it. Place another mirror or piece of glass underneath the candles to catch wax drips.

- Purchase a tea light fireplace log set.

- Purchase or download a wood-burning fireplace DVD to watch on your television.

- Purchase an electric fireplace.

SOUNDS & SCENTS

Sounds:

During Dinner:

Love songs, love songs and more love songs: Gladys Knight and the Pips' "You're the Best Thing that Ever Happen to Me," Kenny Chesney's "You Had Me from Hello," The Eagles' "The Best of My Love," Lady Antebellum's "I Run to You," Rascal Flatts' I Melt," Bette Midler's "Wind Beneath My Wings," James Blunt's "You're Beautiful," Hoobastank's "The Reason," Josh Groban's *Awake* CD, Mariah Carey's *Mariah — The Ballads* CD, Anita Baker's *Rapture* CD, Phil Collins' *Love Songs a compilation… old and new* CD.

After Dinner:

Steamy love songs: The Righteous Brothers' "Unchained Melody," Faith Hill's "Let's Make Love," Berlin's "Take My Breath Away," Billy Currington's "Must Be Doing Something Right," Chris Young's "Gettin' You Home," Ty Herndon's "No Mercy," Barry White's *All-Time Greatest Hits* CD, Marvin Gaye's *Number 1's* CD.

For more love songs go to *nowthatsromantic.com*.

Scents:

Rose, Strawberry, Cashmere

WHAT TO WEAR

Women:

- Pink or red bra and panties set
- Traditional pink or red Valentine negligee, teddy or corset
- Pink or red cocktail dress

Accessorize with pearl or diamond earrings and necklaces, pink or red nail polish, eyelashes, garter belt, silk stockings, clear, pink or red crystal heart-shaped tattoo and heels or stilettos.

Men:

- Pink or red open dress shirt with black or grey dress pants
- Pink or red open casual shirt with blue or black jeans
- Boxer shorts: red silk or white silk with red hearts or lips

HOW TO MAKE YOUR HEART-SHAPED FUR RUG

Faux fur can be found at most fabric stores. Fold the fur lengthwise with the fur facing inside. Hold together with straight pins. As shown on the diagram below, sketch half a heart on the back of the fabric. Cut out heart, remove pins and unfold. To remove excess fur, toss the fur in the dryer on a delicate setting for about five minutes. Remove promptly and shake vigorously to fluff. Do not skip the excess fur removal process, or you will have fur fibers in your mouth, eyes, food etc.

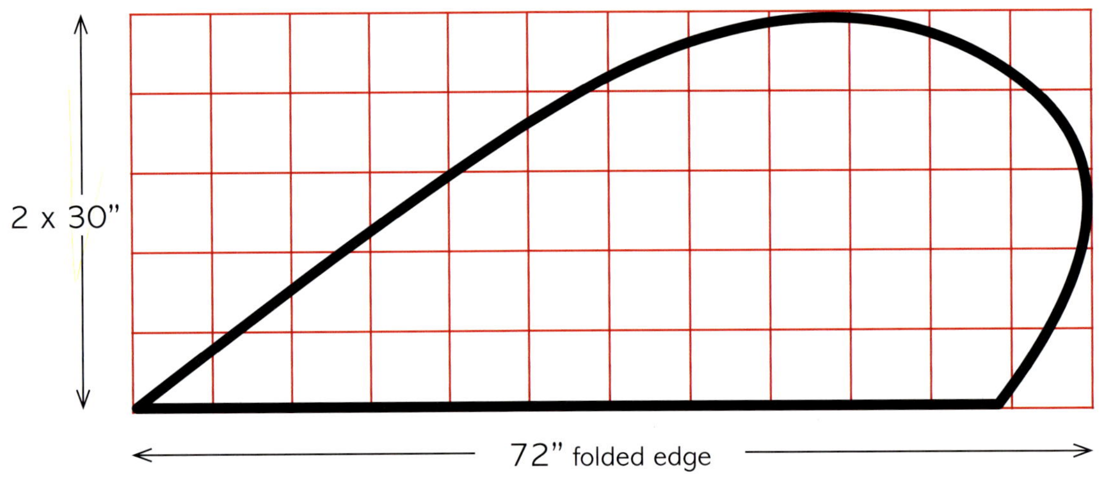

Heart dimensions:

folded fabric: width 30" x length 72", (60" x 72" flat) each square = 6 inches

To download and print template, go to **nowthatsromantic.com**

Now That's
Romantic!

Surrender The Booty!

*Could anything be as venturesome
as dining with the likes of a pirate?
Notorious, charming, free spirits are they.
They indulge in food and drink
amassed from royalty and sit among
lavish mayhem. All around a bounty of
dripping jewels, pearls and plunder glitter
and gleam in the candlelight.
Aye, a pirate's life for me!*

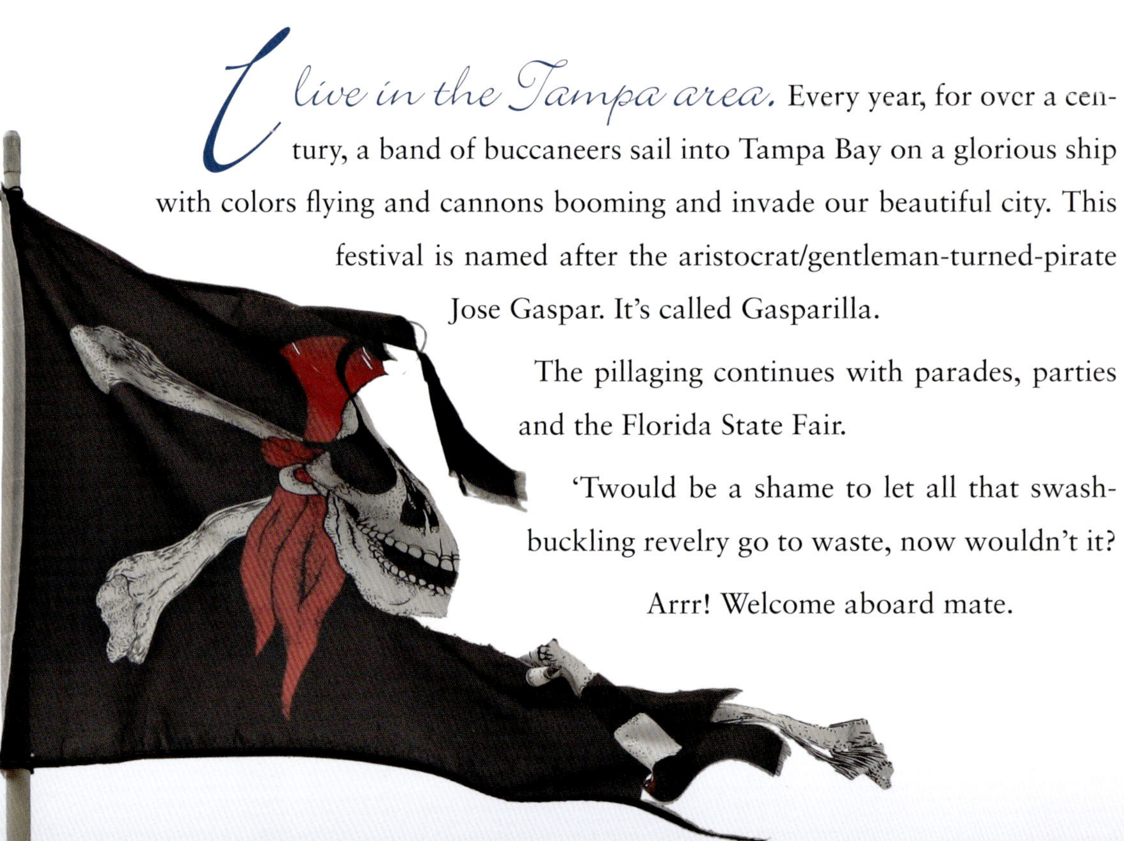

Photo courtesy of EventFest, Inc., Tampa, FL

I live in the Tampa area. Every year, for over a century, a band of buccaneers sail into Tampa Bay on a glorious ship with colors flying and cannons booming and invade our beautiful city. This festival is named after the aristocrat/gentleman-turned-pirate Jose Gaspar. It's called Gasparilla.

The pillaging continues with parades, parties and the Florida State Fair.

'Twould be a shame to let all that swash-buckling revelry go to waste, now wouldn't it?

Arrr! Welcome aboard mate.

THINGS YOU'LL NEED

- [ ] 2½ yards navy crushed-velvet fabric for tablecloth
- [ ] 1-1½ yards jewel-toned, gold-embroidered brocade fabric for table, optional
- [ ] 2 ornate, antique-like plates, salad bowls and dessert/bread plates
- [ ] 2 gold chargers or antique-like placemats
- [ ] 2 sets of flatware
- [ ] 2 ivory lace-trimmed napkins
- [ ] 2 gold-rimmed wine glasses
- [ ] 2 silver, pewter or crystal champagne goblets
- [ ] 2 silver, pewter or crystal champagne flutes, optional
- [ ] 1 wrought-iron candelabra
- [ ] White taper candles for candelabra
- [ ] 4 gold votive candleholders
- [ ] 4 white votive candles for candleholders
- [ ] 2 boxes (144 count each) of gold, silver, pearl and colorful parade beads
- [ ] 144 gold coins or doubloons
- [ ] 80-100 large faux diamonds, rubies, sapphires, topaz and emeralds
- [ ] Miscellaneous assortment of silver: goblets, cream and sugar sets, platters, candlesticks, etc.
- [ ] Miscellaneous assortment of costume jewelry: pearls, gold chains, broaches and rings with large colorful gemstones, tiaras, etc.
- [ ] Flicker-flame light bulbs for chandelier
- [ ] 2 large tassel tiebacks for chair backs, optional
- [ ] 1 large tree, optional
- [ ] 1 up light, optional
- [ ] Tart warmer, optional
- [ ] Scented tart, cube or wax chips, optional

Surrender
The Booty!

- ☐ 2 dark, wooden pillar candleholders
- ☐ 2 white pillar candles for candleholders
- ☐ 2 votive candleholders
- ☐ 2 votive candles

This roomscape is all about rogue extravagance. It's a perfect example of how a simple idea presented in mass can produce dramatic results.

To give your plastic plunder a more authentic look, rummage through your house in search of anything that resembles treasure: costume jewelry, silver pieces such as goblets, candlesticks, cream and sugar scts, platters etc. Then mingle it in with the fake stuff.

If you have a china cabinet, turn the lights on and display your sparkling loot. Fill clear glasses with gemstones, scatter doubloons, drape beads from knobs, bowls etc.

Let's Put It Together

TABLE SETTING

- Drape the navy crushed-velvet fabric on the table.

- Set each place with chargers/placemats, dishes, flatware and glassware.

- Pinch the center of each napkin, partially roll the pinched end and tuck into the wine glasses with the lace fanning out the top of the glass.

- Place a goblet in the center of each place setting.

- Scrunch and place the brocade fabric opposite the place settings, optional.

- Place the wrought-iron candelabra on the brocade fabric.

- Place the votive candles around the table.

- Hang and drape the beads, starting with the chandelier and candelabra.

- Scatter the beads, gemstones and doubloons throughout the table.

- Mix the silver pieces and costume jewelry into your plunder.

- Fill the goblets on the plates with doubloons, gemstones and beads allowing them to spill onto the plate.

- Attach the tassel tiebacks to the chair backs, optional.

73

DÉCOR & LIGHTING

- Hang and drape the beads from the china cabinet, chair backs, doorknobs, draperies etc.

- Place the up light under and behind the tree, optional.

- Toss treasure on the floor as if it spilled off of the table.

- Place the pillar candleholders and votive candleholders on cart/buffet, optional.

- Scatter additional treasure on the cart/buffet, optional.

SOUNDS & SCENTS

Sounds:

During Dinner:
Any of the *Pirates of the Caribbean* Soundtrack CDs

After Dinner:
Bad boy rock: AC/DC's "You Shook Me All Night Long," Def Leppard's "Pour Some Sugar on Me," The Rolling Stone's "Brown Sugar," Van Halen's "Feel Your Love Tonight," Aerosmith's *The Essential: Aerosmith* CD, Bon Jovi's *Greatest Hits – The Ultimate Collection* CD, Led Zeppelin's *Mothership (Remastered)* CD, Nickelback, Soundgarden, Shinedown, Bush

Scents:

Ocean, Citrus, Clove

WHAT TO WEAR

Women:

- Pirate costume

- Lady Admiral Pirate: Navy-style jacket and mini skirt with bra and panties set

- Wench: Off-the-shoulder peasant top, corset, wench skirt

Accessorize with dangling or large hoop earrings, pearls and chains, large gemstone rings, pirate hat (with or without an ostrich feather), hair in an up-do with a long ponytail extension to one side, jeweled hair comb (with or without an ostrich feather), eyelashes, fishnet hose, black knee-high stiletto boots.

For an easy no-sew wench skirt, go to *nowthatsromantic.com*.

Men:

- Pirate costume

- White pirate shirt and black jeans

Accessorize with pirate hat (with or without an ostrich feather), bandana on your head, a single hoop earring, eye-patch, beads, large gemstone ring, waist sash and boots.

Adapt this roomscape into a Halloween Ghost Ship by simply adding spider webs, skulls, skeletons and sea fog. (See One Haunted Evening for spider web and fog tips.)

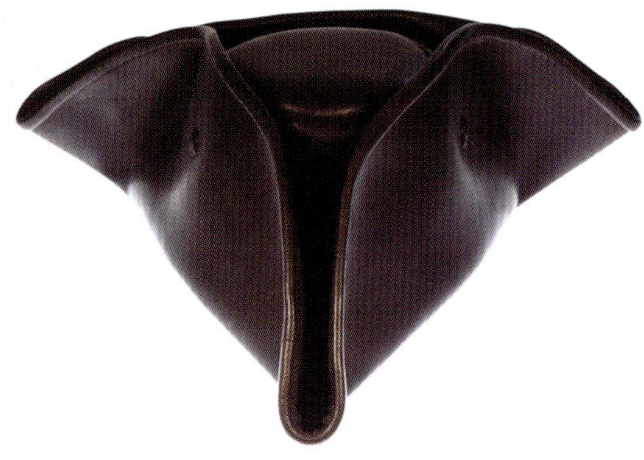

Secluded Safari

Journey to a place where leopard,
elephant and giraffe roam free.
Where an enormous gold sun melts into
the Serengeti and enchanting tribal
music resonates through the bush.
In your lodge, candles radiate from
within a sheer white, mosquito net
canopy—transforming your bed into a
breathtaking luminescent chamber.
Exotic animal skins and native
delicacies draw you into the net
like a moth to a flame.
Only this time… you're the game.

osquito nets are the epitome of romance. They're surreal and seductive.

This expedition is not for the timid. It's for the adventurous spirit longing to explore and unleash primal passions. Whether you're the *predator* or the *prey*, you'll find the thrill of the hunt exhilarating and provocative.

Set your net… lure them in… then ambush your trophy.

You see, when on safari, the wildlife isn't always outdoors.

THINGS YOU'LL NEED

- [ ] 1 dark bamboo, wooden or wicker bed tray
- [ ] Palm leaf placemat or real palm leaves
- [ ] 2 forks
- [ ] 2 zebra napkins or bandanas, or ½ yard of zebra fabric
- [ ] 2 dark wooden or bamboo napkin rings
- [ ] 2 black, dark wooden or brown plates
- [ ] 1-2 African violets or red/pink hibiscus
- [ ] 2 green lowball glasses, beer mugs or stemless wine glasses
- [ ] Four-corner mosquito net kit
- [ ] Small nails, thumbtacks or staple gun
- [ ] White cord or twine, needed for ceilings higher than 8 feet
- [ ] 1 small black, 4-6 votive, wrought-iron candle chandelier
- [ ] 4-6 battery operated votive candles for candle chandelier
- [ ] Black chain (1-3 feet) length depends on your ceiling height
- [ ] 1 medium white teacup hook
- [ ] 1 small anchor, optional
- [ ] White or off-white sheets and pillowcases
- [ ] 2 yards faux leopard or tiger skin
- [ ] 1-3 black fur pillows, optional
- [ ] Bench or bedside tray table, optional
- [ ] 1yard faux cheetah skin for bench or bedside tray table, optional
- [ ] 1 lantern, preferably a tea light version, optional
- [ ] 1 white candle/tea light for lantern, optional
- [ ] 1 or more palm trees
- [ ] 1 up light, optional
- [ ] Floral wire
- [ ] Tart warmer, optional
- [ ] Scented tart, cube or wax chips, optional

TABLE SETTING

- If making the zebra napkins, cut the fabric into 16-inch squares.

- Pinch the napkins in the center and pull through the napkin rings.

- Set the tray with palm leaf placemats/real palm leaves, plates, forks, napkins and flower. Set aside.

- Drape the cheetah skin on the bench or bedside tray table, optional.

- Place the lantern on the bench or bedside tray table, optional. Set aside.

DÉCOR & LIGHTING

- Locate and mark the center point of the bed on the ceiling with a pencil.

- Insert anchor (optional) and teacup hook into the center point. Hang the black chain from the hook.

- Stretch out the mosquito net on the bed, aligning the shorter sides of the net with the head and foot of the bed. Raise the corners of the net to the ceiling and attach using kit hardware, small nails, thumbtacks or staple gun. If your ceiling is higher than 8 feet, add white cord to each corner tab. Add enough length to allow the net to puddle on the floor by 3-4 inches.

- Attach the candle chandelier to the black chain at desired height.

- Cut two 8-inch pieces of floral wire.

- Find the inside center point of one canopy panel and thread the floral wire through that point. Raise that point of the panel above the chandelier and twist tie the panel to the chain at desired height. Repeat for the other side. The canopy should peak higher in the center, than at the four corners. (See photo on page 85.)

- Using the tiebacks in the mosquito net kit, tie the *side* panels to the corners.

- Place the *battery operated* votive candles in chandelier. **(DO NOT use real candles inside the mosquito net.)**

- Cut the faux fur in the shape of a tiger or leopard hide. (See Faux Hide Template page 84.)

- Lay the faux hide on the diagonal across the bed.

- Arrange the black pillows at the head of the bed.

- Place the bedside tray table or bench close to the bed to accommodate drinks, optional.

- Place the lantern on the bench or bedside tray table, optional.

- Position the palm trees, optional.

- Place the up lights under and behind the palm trees, optional.

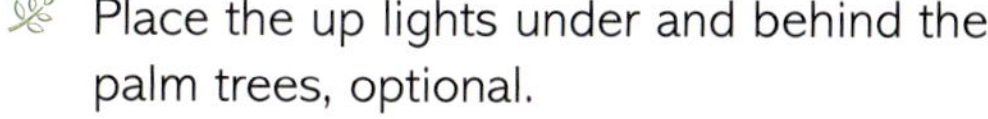

SOUNDS & SCENTS

Sounds:

During dinner:

African wildlife sounds mixed with instrumental tribal music: African Tribal Orchestra's *African Dream Lounge* CDs, Volumes, I, II and III

After dinner:

Afrika's *Song of the Tribal Spirit* CD, Steve Millington's *African Voices N' Chant Nguru* CD, Brent Lewis' *Drum Sex or Earth Tribe Rhythms* CD

Scents:

Musk, Myrrh, Floral

FAUX HIDE TEMPLATE

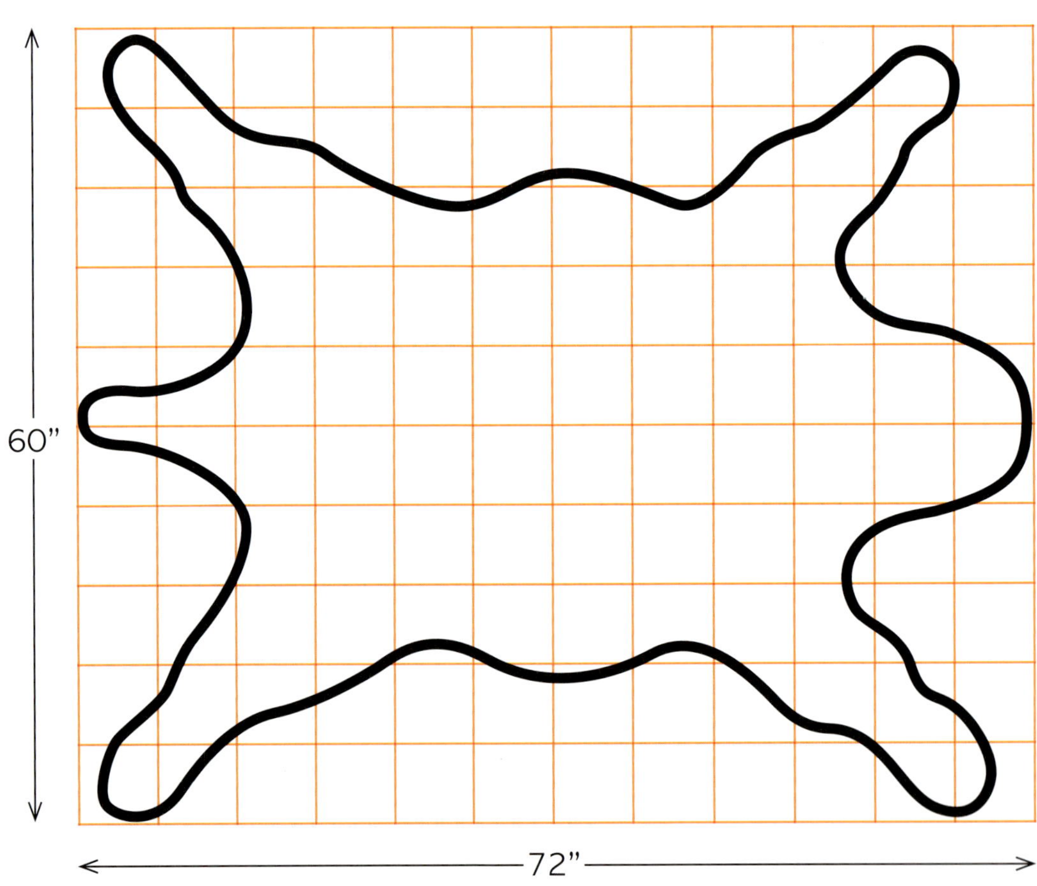

Faux hide dimensions:

fabric: width 60" x length 72", each square = 6 inches

To download and print template, go to ***nowthatsromantic.com***

Now That's
Romantic!

Mosquito Net Short Cuts

Most mosquito net kits come complete with instructions, tiebacks and mounting hardware. But because the nets are practically weightless, and it will probably only be up a day or two, consider using a staple gun instead of the mounting hardware. A couple of staples on each corner should do the trick. The staples are easily removed with a pair of needle-nose pliers and the holes are virtually undetectable.

If you have a tall, four-poster bed like I do, don't bother attaching the corners to the ceiling, simply drape the corners of the net over the posters.

Secluded
Safari

WHAT TO WEAR

Women:

- Jane/Warrior Woman: (See How to Make No-Sew Warrior Woman Costume at *nowthatsromantic.com*.)

- Leopard or tiger print lingerie or bra and panties set

- The Hunter: Safari-style mini dress, wide leather belt, safari hat, leopard heels

- The Prey: Exotic cat suit, smoky cat eye make-up, mane-like hair, black claw nails

Accessorize with wild tousled hair, hair extensions, feather hair extensions, leather laces or cording wrapped around locks of hair, eyelashes, primitive bone jewelry or beads, arm cuff bracelets, lace-up-to-the-knee leather sandals or bare feet with anklets, temporary body tattoos or markings, black thigh-high fishnet hosiery, bronze make-up, a tan: real, lotion or spray-on, bronze shimmer body lotion, a fake spear.

Men:

- Tarzan: faux leopard skin cut into sarong, fake hip knife (For instructions to make sarong, see How to Make No-Sew Warrior Woman Costume at *nowthatsromantic.com*.)

- Hunter: Cotton safari shirt with cargo or khaki shorts, safari-style hat and sandals

Jungle Fare

- Serve appetizer food in bite-size pieces that can be eaten with your fingers or a fork. Avoid drippy messy foods.

- When choosing glassware, use stemless, bottom heavy glasses. Martini and wine glasses are too unstable for bed dining.

Now That's
Romantic!

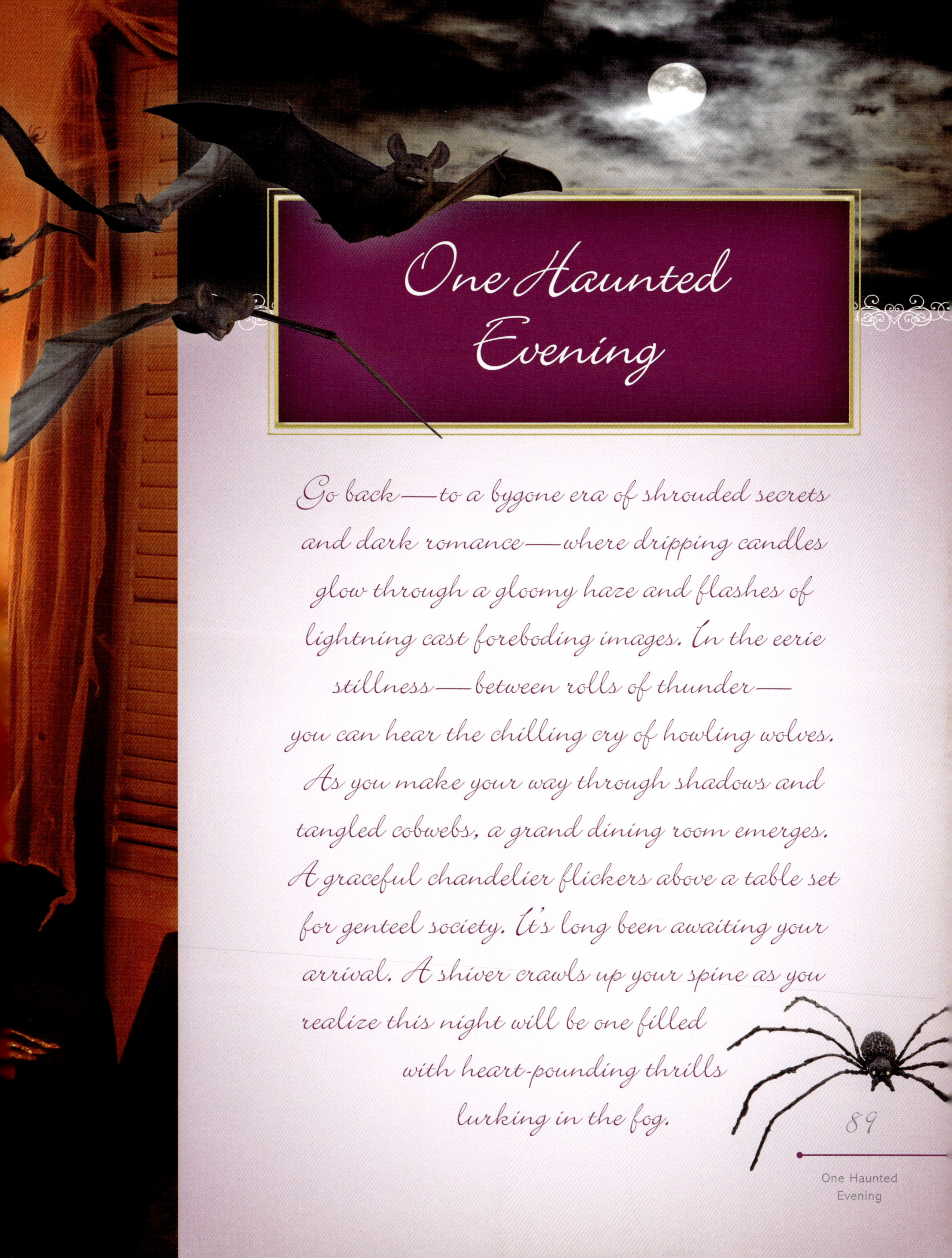

One Haunted Evening

Go back—to a bygone era of shrouded secrets and dark romance—where dripping candles glow through a gloomy haze and flashes of lightning cast foreboding images. In the eerie stillness—between rolls of thunder—you can hear the chilling cry of howling wolves. As you make your way through shadows and tangled cobwebs, a grand dining room emerges. A graceful chandelier flickers above a table set for genteel society. It's long been awaiting your arrival. A shiver crawls up your spine as you realize this night will be one filled with heart-pounding thrills lurking in the fog.

Several years ago, shortly before Halloween, I purchased an inexpensive fog machine. My intentions were to create a spooky porch greeting for our neighborhood ghosts and goblins. But, being the curious and impatient person that I am, I couldn't wait to get it home and see how it worked. Within minutes, I had it assembled and turned on. Moments later the fog began to flow…. and so did my imagination.

Shame on me. Trick-or-treaters. What trick-or-treaters? I had just discovered a new trick of my own. And Doug was my unsuspecting victim.

It's mysterious, it's erotic—and *it's our favorite!*

THINGS YOU'LL NEED

- ☐ 2½ yards black fabric or tablecloth
- ☐ 2 elegant chargers or lace placemats
- ☐ 2 antique-like plates, salad bowls and bread plates
- ☐ 2 sets of antique-like flatware or silverware
- ☐ 2 ivory lace-edged napkins
- ☐ 2 silver napkin rings
- ☐ 2 crystal water glasses, optional
- ☐ 2 crystal or silver wine and/or champagne goblets
- ☐ 2 small lace doilies, optional
- ☐ 2 tarnished silver candelabras
- ☐ Long white taper candles for candelabras
- ☐ 1 dead rose arrangement
- ☐ 2 dead long-stemmed roses
- ☐ Flicker-flame light bulbs, one for each socket of your chandelier
- ☐ 1 large bag of spider webs
- ☐ Lots of spiders or spider rings (Cut the rings off.)
- ☐ Clear thumbtacks or staple gun with a wire guide attachment
- ☐ 1 fog machine with timer
- ☐ 1 small container of fog juice
- ☐ Creepy Cloth, Freaky Fabric or cheesecloth, optional
- ☐ 1 6-8 foot dead tree branch, optional
- ☐ 1 12-inch decorative plant pot or urn, optional
- ☐ Rocks or dirt to fill decorative pot or urn, optional
- ☐ 1 up light, optional
- ☐ 1 25-watt amber light bulb for up light, optional
- ☐ 1–2 pounds of dry ice, broken into pieces, optional
- ☐ Ice bucket or cauldron, optional
- ☐ Tart warmer, optional
- ☐ Scented tart, cube or wax chips, optional

One Haunted
Evening

Let's Put It Together

TABLE SETTING

- Drape the black fabric or tablecloth on the table.

- Set each place with chargers/placemats, dishes, flatware and glassware.

- Pinch the center of the napkins and pull through the napkin rings.

- Slide the stem of the dead roses through the napkin rings on the top of the napkins. Cut stems to desired length. Center on the plates.

- Place the flower arrangement in the middle of the table.

- Flank the silver candelabras on each side of the flower arrangement with optional lace doilies underneath.

- For room fog, pour the fog juice in the fog machine and set up behind a sofa, chair or in an inconspicuous spot.

- Adjust the fog machine timer to the desired fog amount.

- For table fog (at the last minute) put warm water in your drink glasses, cauldron or ice bucket. Then, **using tongs or gloves**, add small pieces of dry ice to the warm water, optional**.** (See Fog Safety Tips page 93.)

Fog Safety Tips

FOG MACHINES

- Fog machines produce heat, so keep them a safe distance from fabrics. As a precaution, place your fog machine on a cookie sheet, this will keep it off the carpet and catch any accidental fog juice spills or drips.

- Some smoke detectors are fog sensitive, so don't place them too close to smoke detectors.

DRY ICE

- When working with dry ice: **NEVER** handle with your bare hands. **ALWAYS** use tongs or cloth gloves to prevent contact with skin. **NEVER** taste or put dry ice in your mouth.

- It's okay to serve your drinks with a small piece of dry ice, but do not consume until the dry ice has completely evaporated.

Recycle Old Stuff

- My florist thought I was crazy when I tried to order a dead flower arrangement. So plan ahead and order your flowers a month or so in advance or if you know someone who has received roses ask if you can have them after they're dead.

- Thrift stores are a terrific resource for this roomscape: old tablecloths, lace curtains, silver, dishes, glassware, etc. If it's tattered, yellowed or tarnished, that's even better. It's also a great place to find costume ideas.

- Go green and cheap.

DÉCOR & LIGHTING

- Place the flicker-flame light bulbs in the chandelier.

- If using a dead tree, remove live or silk trees from the room.

- Plant the dead tree in pot or urn with dirt or rocks.

- Attach the spider webs to the chandelier, tree, flowers, candelabras etc.

- Attach the spiders to the webs.

- Place the up light under and behind the dead tree.

- Hang the creepy cloth in doorways or windows with
  clear thumbtacks, optional.

SPIDER WEBS

No haunted house is complete without cobwebs. They're inexpensive and can be found anywhere Halloween decorations are sold. Wrap them around chandeliers, candelabras, flowers, etc. Dangle lonely spiders from a single strand or create an ominous entrance by partially obstructing doorways.

Attaching webs to your walls and ceilings can be a challenge. If you can get a volunteer to help you stretch the webs, it will be a much easier task. The best way I have found to attach them to walls and ceilings is with clear/white thumbtacks or a staple gun with a wire guide.

The secret to making spider webs look realistic is to split, stretch, snag and staple one continuous piece of webbing in as many different directions as possible. If it clumps, stretch it from a different angle and snag it or staple it on to something else. The thinner you stretch it, the eerier it looks.

For tips on how to make Lightning on Demand go to *nowthatsromantic.com.*

SOUNDS & SCENTS

Sounds:

During dinner:

Thunder and lightning, howling wolves, wind and eerie music: Drew's *Famous Fright Flicks* a 2 CD set, *Halloween Music Specialist* CD

After dinner:

Drew's *Famous Halloween Party Music* CD, additional tunes: The Eagles' "Witchy Woman," Santana's "Black Magic Woman," Alice Cooper's "Welcome to My Nightmare," Blue Oyster Cult's "Don't Fear the Reaper," Michael Jackson's "Thriller," George Thorogood's "Bad to the Bone," Warren Zevon's "Werewolves of London"

Scents:

Rose, Lilac, Lily of the Valley

WHAT TO WEAR

Women:

- Ghost/Zombie: Age and tatter any dress, gown, negligee or bridal gown, white or grey hair extensions, ashen make-up with sallow eyes

- Spirit: Flowing off-white or silver-grey tattered hood and cape, matching lingerie, pale make-up, slippers

- Victorian Victim: Sheer Victorian lace robe and negligee, pale make-up, old-fashioned jewelry, eyelashes, banana curls or up-do with a jeweled comb, bare feet or slippers

- Gothic: Black leather or satin lingerie, hooded cape, sleek or spiked jet-black hair, red hair extensions, gothic jewelry, pallid face with heavy black eyeliner, black/red lipstick, black nail polish, torn fishnet hose, black stiletto boots

Men:

- Ghost/Zombie: Aged and tattered clothes, suit or tuxedo, ashen make-up with sunken, sallow eyes

- Vampire: Suit, vest, cumberbund, cape, pale make-up, fangs, large Victorian Ring on forefinger, antique cane

- Werewolf

- The Butler

For tips on How to Make Your Own Creepy Cloth and Age Clothing, go to *nowthatsromantic.com*.

Days after our dinner, I was boxing up the fog machine to store in the attic. Doug walked by and this was his reaction: "Before you pack that away, we should have an encore. In fact, why don't we make it a Halloween tradition?"

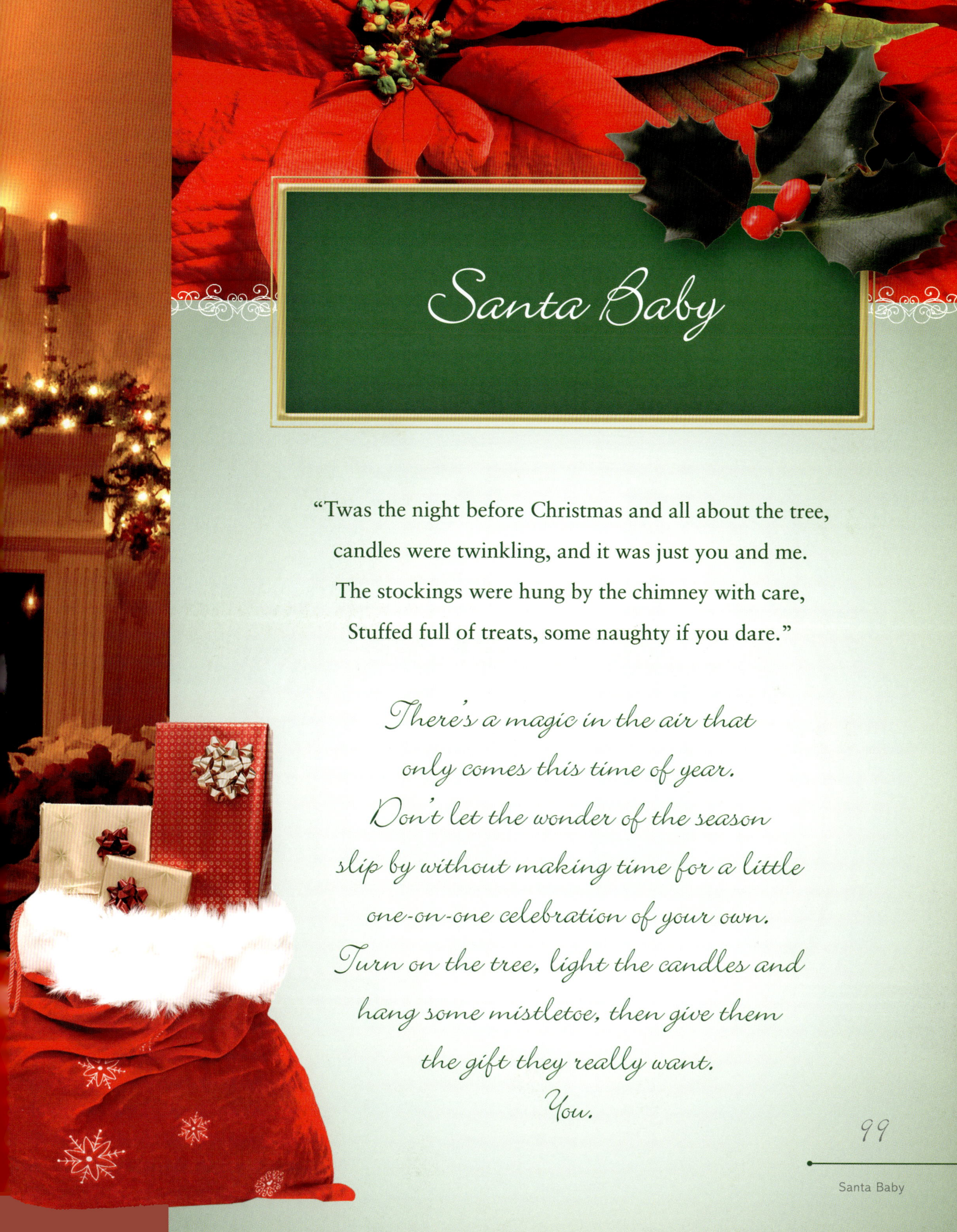

Santa Baby

"Twas the night before Christmas and all about the tree,
candles were twinkling, and it was just you and me.
The stockings were hung by the chimney with care,
Stuffed full of treats, some naughty if you dare."

There's a magic in the air that
only comes this time of year.
Don't let the wonder of the season
slip by without making time for a little
one-on-one celebration of your own.
Turn on the tree, light the candles and
hang some mistletoe, then give them
the gift they really want.
You.

 I'll put a red-velvet bow and white lights on anything and everything—dogs included. Even my cell phone boasts a holiday screen and ring tone. I love the season, but that doesn't make it any less hectic. Parties, shopping, wrapping, baking—in the midst of all the hustle and bustle it's easy to neglect the one we love most. That's why I kept this roomscape simple. Let your tree and holiday décor be your roomscape, set the table, order take-out, then…

"Have Yourself a Merry Little Christmas."

THINGS YOU'LL NEED

- [ ] Small table
- [ ] 2 chairs
- [ ] Red tablecloth or 1½-2 yards red fabric
- [ ] 2 gold chargers or placemats
- [ ] 2 white plates and salad bowls with gold or silver trim
- [ ] 2 sets of flatware
- [ ] 2 red napkins
- [ ] 12-inches of 1-inch black leather or vinyl strap or belting
- [ ] 2 square silver 1-inch buckles
- [ ] Stapler
- [ ] 2 champagne or wine glasses
- [ ] 1 medium black lantern
- [ ] 1 white candle or tea light for lantern
- [ ] 1-2 holly picks or sprays
- [ ] Small red velvet bow
- [ ] Floral wire
- [ ] 1 12-inch round or octagon mirror
- [ ] Small gold and/or silver jingle bells
- [ ] Clear votive candleholders
- [ ] White votive candles for candleholders
- [ ] Mistletoe or mistletoe ball, optional
- [ ] Red ribbon to hang mistletoe, optional
- [ ] Thumbtack, optional
- [ ] Gift-filled stocking, optional
- [ ] Tart warmer, optional
- [ ] Scented tart, cube or wax chips, optional

TABLE SETTING

- Place the table and chairs in front of the Christmas tree.

- Drape the tablecloth or fabric on the table.

- Set the table with chargers/placemats, dishes, flatware and glassware.

- Make Santa belt napkin rings by cutting the black leather strap into two 6-inch pieces. Slide the buckle onto the strap. Overlap the ends of the strap and staple together.

- Fold the napkins in half and roll tightly. Slide the napkin rings on the napkins. Place the napkins in the center of the place settings.

- Position the mirror in the center of the table.

- Using a large piece of floral wire, twist tie the bow and holly together. Then twist tie the bow and holly to the lantern. Trim excess floral wire.

- Put the candle in the lantern and center the lantern on top of the mirror.

- Scatter the jingle bells on the table.

DÉCOR & LIGHTING

- Position the votive candles throughout the room.
- Hang the mistletoe/mistletoe ball using ribbon and a thumbtack to the ceiling above the table, optional.

Fill a stocking with some of your sweetheart's favorite indulgences: dark chocolate, macadamia nuts, a coffee mug, vanilla scented massage oil, chocolate finger paints, love coupon, a favorite magazine, movie, book or CD—gifts sure to melt even Grinch's cold heart.

To download and print the love coupon, go to *nowthatsromantic.com*.

103

Sounds:

During dinner:
Kenny G's *The Greatest Holiday Classics* CD, Scott Hamilton's *Late Night Christmas Eve: Romantic Sax with Strings* CD

After dinner:
Christmas love songs: *Number 1's: Christmas* CD, Harry Connick, Jr.'s *What a Night! – A Christmas Album* CD, individual tunes: Madonna's "Santa Baby," Randy Travis' "Meet Me Under the Mistletoe," Mariah Carey's "All I Want for Christmas is You," John Mellencamp's "I Saw Mommy Kissing Santa Claus"

Scents:

Cinnamon, Cookie, Holly Berry

WHAT TO WEAR

Women:

- Sexy Santa lingerie

- Red cocktail dress

- A Gift: Red satin ribbon and bows, a gift tag necklace and heels (Yes, that's all.)

- Red cat suit: Add white fur collar and cuffs and a Santa belt

- Santa's Helper/Elf lingerie

Accessorize with jingle bell earrings, holly in your hair, sparkle hairspray, eyelashes, Santa hat, red nail polish, red or black stilettos, black knee-high stiletto boots, sparkle body lotion.

WHAT TO WEAR

Men:

- White, red or holiday dress shirt with black dress slacks
- Red flannel or Santa boxer shorts

Accessorize with holiday tie, suspenders or Santa hat.

Now That's
Romantic!

And I heard him exclaim, as he
turned out the lights,

"Merry Christmas to all,
to all lovers, good night!"

So now what's your excuse? It's not only accept-able to host a romantic dinner and not cook, its *en vogue*. If you can order take-out and operate an oven or microwave, you can do this. I'll show you how.

TIPS ON TAKE-OUT

When placing your order, request *all* courses be separated and packed in individual containers. *Especially* sauces. This makes warming, presenta-tion and cleanup a breeze. Ask for extra sauce, salad dressing, butter, etc. Remember to compensate your server for their extra trouble.

Fried foods become limp and unappealing in no time, so unless you live within five to ten minutes of the restaurant, it may be wise to avoid them. But if you've just got to have that fried calamari, like I do, arrive at the restaurant early and pick it up as soon as it's pulled from the fryer. To keep it crisp, crack the container and allow some of the steam to escape. Hurry home, lay it on a foil cookie sheet and pop it in the oven or toaster oven at 225 degrees for about five minutes. Don't be tempted to warm it up in the microwave. That will make it tough and chewy.

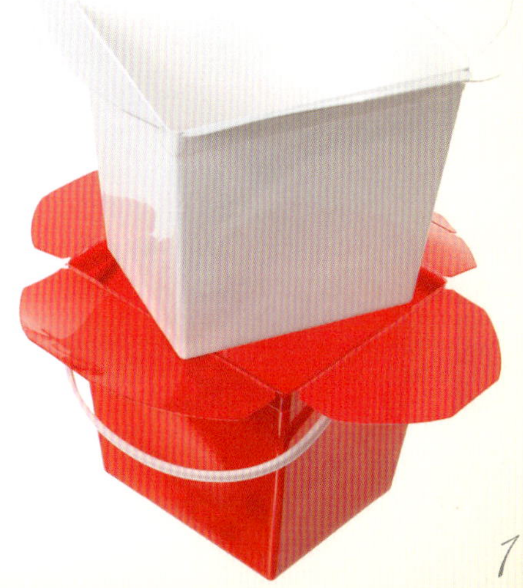

A PRETTY PLATE

With a little effort and a touch of know-how, you can create a meal that's delicious *and* eye-catching. First, arrange food portions in the center of the plate, leaving space between each item. Wipe the rim of the plate of any drips or spills with a damp cloth or paper towel. Last, position your garnish. Never crowd the plate—too much food looks messy.

Garnishes cost pennies and take seconds. I'm not talking about carving radishes and tomatoes into roses. I'm talking about simple touches like; a lemon curl, a sprig of basil, an herb blossom or a pineapple wedge. In the same way a bow is the finishing touch to a gift, these small embellishments will add the finishing touch to your dinner. For additional garnishing ideas go to *nowthatsromantic.com* to download and print our Hassle-Free Garnish Guide.

I'LL TOAST TO THAT

Beverages add a festive flair to any meal. If you don't drink alcohol, substitute sparkling juices, punch or virgin concoctions and serve them in cocktail glasses, garnishes and all. Prepare enough for the entire evening. And don't forget to toast!

Salt isn't the only thing that looks great on the rim of a glass. Bedazzle your beverage with colored sugars, cocoa, cinnamon etc., all of which can be found in the baking section of your local grocery store. The color and flavor of the condiment should complement the color and flavor of the drink.

To decorate a glass with salt, rub a wedge of lime along the rim. Then dip the rim into a small plate of salt. To decorate with sugar, dip the rim in

a small plate of corn syrup, then in a small plate of sugar, cocoa, shredded coconut etc. Prepare the glasses in advance then chill and store in the refrigerator or freezer.

If serving champagne, martinis, white wine or sparkling juices, garnish with frozen fruit. They not only add panache, they pull double duty by keeping them cold without watering them down. For more drink ideas, go to ***nowthatsromantic.com*** and download and print the Beverage Garnishing Guide.

A SNAPPY CLEANUP

If you're baking or warming food in the oven or microwave, invest in disposable bakeware. This gives you the option to cover and save your leftovers in the container you cooked it in or, if you don't want the headache, toss it all in the trash.

Empty your dishwasher on the morning of your dinner. When it's all over, it'll be ready to take on the few items you have left.

KEEP IT LIGHT

Remember, you are hosting a romantic dinner, *not* a Thanksgiving feast. How do you feel after Thanksgiving—after you've indulged in turkey and stuffing, mashed potatoes and gravy, squash casserole, green beans and pecan pie? Are you miserable? Bloated? Lethargic? Is indigestion setting in? Or are you frisky, passionate and ready to *get it on*?

Bottom line—when serving a romantic dinner, *keep your portions small*, especially when serving several courses. You want to be unfastening buttons and belts after dinner, but *not* because you pigged out.

FINAL THOUGHTS

If this is uncharted territory for you, don't let it intimidate you. Start small. Do as much or as little as you're comfortable with. Start somewhere, then do a little more each time. The only way you can fail is if you don't try. Will it take some effort? Sure. What party doesn't? But you're worth it.

All relationships need a boost now and then, so go for it! Have fun. Escape reality. Rediscover the love of your youth. You'll both win.

"When you give each other everything, it becomes an even trade. Each wins all."

LOIS MCMASTER BOJOLD

YOU MATTER

Nothing would tickle me more than to hear from you. I hope to be your source of romantic inspiration, laughter and lasting memories for many years. Please visit my website at *nowthatsromantic.com* and share your suggestions and experiences—what worked and what didn't. I'd love to hear your ideas and success stories. With your input, I can focus on the things that matter most to you.

112

14
Hot Date!
13
8
15
16

Time Line

3 WEEKS OUT

- ☐ Give an invitation, if applicable.
- ☐ Pick up a take-out menu and highlight your choices or plan a menu.
- ☐ Start a grocery list. (Don't forget disposable bakeware.)
- ☐ Gather items you already have for table setting and roomscape.
- ☐ Make a Table Setting and Roomscape List of items you need to buy.
- ☐ Buy a fire extinguisher, if necessary.
- ☐ Make babysitting arrangements for children, teens or pets.

2 WEEKS OUT

- ☐ Purchase items on your Table Setting and Roomscape List.
- ☐ Preview your table setting. Store.
- ☐ Prepare or preview as much of your roomscape as possible. Store.

1 WEEK OUT

- ☐ Prepare your play list or purchase music.
- ☐ Prepare or purchase your attire.
- ☐ Prepare or purchase something for your spouse to wear, optional.
- ☐ Clean the rooms you will be using.
- ☐ Put lights in the trees or greenery, if applicable.
- ☐ Order flowers. Florist phone # _______________________________
- ☐ Try on your entire outfit, including accessories. Store.
- ☐ Buy a card or gift, if applicable.

2-3 DAYS OUT

- ☐ Get a haircut or color.
- ☐ Get a manicure, pedicure or bikini wax, optional.
- ☐ Drop off dry cleaning.
- ☐ Do grocery shopping, if applicable.

DAY BEFORE

- ☐ Wash your bed linens.
- ☐ Touch up the room, if necessary.
- ☐ Prepare make-ahead foods, if applicable.
- ☐ Prepare garnishes, lemon slices, freeze berries etc.
- ☐ Mix drinks, if applicable.
- ☐ Pick up dry cleaning.
- ☐ Place your fire extinguisher.

DAY OF YOUR DINNER

Morning:

- ☐ Empty your dishwasher.
- ☐ Set up music; CD player, iPOD, computer, etc.
- ☐ Pick up your flower arrangement, if applicable.
- ☐ Set up the roomscape.
- ☐ Set the table.

Afternoon:

- ☐ Take your children, teens or pets to the sitter, if applicable.
- ☐ Order take-out or prepare food. Restaurant phone # ______________________
- ☐ Relax and unwind; bubble bath, massage, pedicure, nap…
- ☐ Get dressed.
- ☐ Set out card or gift, if applicable.

Last Minute:

- ☐ Pick up take-out, if applicable.
- ☐ Turn on props: fog machines, lights in trees, up lights etc.
- ☐ Draw blinds and shades, if applicable.
- ☐ Turn on music.
- ☐ Light candles.
- ☐ Set out appetizers.
- ☐ Pour drinks.

To download and print the Time Line, go to *nowthatsromantic.com.*

CARIBBEAN CABANA

- White cotton panels: Walmart
- Tortoise shell chargers: Pier I Imports
- Silk orchids: JoAnn Fabric and Craft Stores
- Round mosquito net kit: SCS Ltd., *scs-mall.com*

HEARTS ON FIRE

- White faux fur: JoAnn Fabrics
- Fondue Pot: *bedbathandbeyond.com*
- Silk rose petals: JoAnn Fabric and Craft Stores, Michaels and Walmart
- Rose arrangement: Rose at Tiger Lilli's Florist, Lutz, FL (813) 948-0247

SURRENDER THE BOOTY!

- Crushed velvet fabric: JoAnn Fabric and Craft Stores
- Brocade fabric: JoAnn Fabric and Craft Stores
- Wrought-iron candelabra: Thrift store
- Gold votive candleholders: Big Lots!
- Faux coins/doubloons, beads and gemstones: *centurynovelty.com*

SECLUDED SAFARI

- Zebra napkin fabric: JoAnn Fabric and Craft Stores
- Faux leopard and tiger skin: JoAnn Fabric and Craft Stores
- Black plates: Bed Bath and Beyond
- Four-corner mosquito net kit: SCS, Ltd., *scs-mall.com*
- Wrought-iron candle chandelier: *amazon.com*
- Black fur pillows: Ross Dress for Less

ONE HAUNTED EVENING

- Black fabric: JoAnn Fabric and Craft Stores
- Dead flower arrangement: Rose at Tiger Lilli's Florist, Lutz, FL (813) 948-0247
- Fog machine and timer: Walmart
- Old silver: Thrift stores

SANTA BABY

- Lantern: Goodwill
- Champagne glasses: Old Time Pottery
- Black vinyl strap and buckles: JoAnn Fabric and Crafts Stores
- Mistletoe Ball: Target

About the Author

Kim Moore has an insatiable appetite for fun, parties and surprises. An interior decorator by trade, married to her high school sweetheart of thirty-four years and the mother of two grown boys, she understands the pressures of juggling a career, little league, housework and romance. She also recognizes the fact that not everyone is creative or has time to be. That's why she developed the innovative new concept of putting romantic entertaining and decorating ideas into themed, organized packages.

Her faith is what inspired her to keep her marriage young and vibrant. "It's sad so many people have the misconception that Christians are prudes. I want people to say, 'I don't know what they've got, but whatever it is, I want it.'"

Kim and her husband Doug live in Florida.